Hamlyn all-colour paperbacks

Alec A. Purves FRNS

Orders and Decorations

Hamlyn · London
Sun Books · Melbourne

FOREWORD

Orders and decorations exist in nearly every country in the world, and have a history spanning some eight centuries. Consequently in a single small volume it is necessary to be both selective and brief.

This is not intended to be a handbook for the expert, but rather an introductory guide for both the interested public and the beginner or potential collector. It will be found that some countries have been dealt with in fuller detail than others, while some have been omitted altogether. In making our selection we have taken account of several factors; some countries are always popular with collectors, such as the old German states, yet very little information is available in English; others are either unpopular or both insignia and authoritative information are difficult to obtain; in some of the emergent nations orders have been created but the statutes (and insignia) have been changed several times already, while a *coup d'état* often means the abolition of a newly created order and a replacement which itself may last only for a few months. Consequently we have thought it better to include, in the main, the older orders and some well-established modern awards, which are likely to be available to collectors.

As regards the illustrations, it has not been thought practical to quote dimensions, or to keep to a uniform scale of size; some orders have existed for centuries, and thus it is not surprising that the sizes and details of design have varied over the years. In many countries recipients have to buy their insignia, and those offered for sale frequently vary both in size, minor detail, and quality of workmanship.

The author would like to acknowledge with thanks the assistance readily given by Dr K. G. Klietmann (of Berlin), Mr W. G. C. Webb, editor of the Journal of the Orders & Medals Research Society, Spink & Son, Ltd., of London, and Messrs J. B. Hayward & Son, of London.

A.A.P.

Published by The Hamlyn Publishing Group Limited
London · New York · Sydney · Toronto
Hamlyn House, Feltham, Middlesex, England
In association with Sun Books Pty Ltd Melbourne

ISBN 0 600 36708 8
Photoset by BAS Printers Limited, Wallop, Hampshire
Colour separations by Schwitter Limited, Zurich
Printed in Holland by Smeets, Weert

CONTENTS

THE ORIGINS OF ORDERS OF KNIGHTHOOD

It is often difficult to separate legend from history, but there is no doubt that the great religious orders of the tenth and eleventh centuries – brotherhoods of monks who had chosen to live according to a code or *order* – influenced or even founded associated brotherhoods of knights, particularly in connection with the Crusades. These were not only for their own protection but also to fight for the Christian religion.

In the same way that a brotherhood of monks became known as an Order, so the bands of knights adopted the same name. Among the earliest of these was the Order of Knights Templars, founded in AD 1118 as a fighting order, but later extended to include hospital services. The Order of St John of Jerusalem, on the other hand, was founded at approximately the same time, as a hospital order in Jerusalem, but later also took up military duties in protecting pilgrims and participating in Crusades. In AD 1291 they had to leave the Holy Land, and eventually came to Malta, thus becoming known as the Knights of Malta. Today the Order of St John

Monks of an early religious Order

A Knight of Malta and a Knight Templar (from an old German print)

of Jerusalem flourishes independently in many countries, including Britain, but is quite separate from the essentially Roman Catholic body, the Sovereign Military Order of Malta, although they all use very similar insignia and basically they have very similar objects.

Another early foundation, originating in Jerusalem, was the Teutonic Order. Dating from 1190, it was attached to the German *Mariens Hospital*; eventually moving to Marienburg, in Prussia, the Order became very powerful, both in military and political affairs, but later these declined, and in the present century it has returned to hospital and charitable works.

In modern times it has become common usage to describe the *insignia* of these brotherhoods as 'The Order of . . . ', but strictly speaking one should say, for example, 'the *Grand Cross* of the Order of Leopold' or 'the *badge of a Companion* of the Order of the Bath.'

During the middle ages many sovereign princes founded orders of chivalry or knighthood, some of which were actively military in object, while others were instituted as a means of rewarding meritorious services. Thus membership of an order was not necessarily an indication of following a prescribed way of life, but often a visible token of having been recognized for certain virtues – civil as well as military.

Among the early military orders, those founded in Spain and Portugal, in the struggles against the Moors, were perhaps the most important. The Military Order of Aviz, founded in 1162, and the Order of Alcantara (1156); the Military Order of Christ (1319) and the Order of Calatrava (1158); and the Order of St James of the Sword (1170 in Spain, and 1177 in Portugal) – these were the powerful ones, and they formed the pattern for many later foundations.

In England, King Edward III instituted the Order of the Garter, almost certainly in 1348, as a brotherhood of the flower of military manhood; most of the twenty-five original Knights-Companions were young men, and many had fought with the King and the Black Prince at Crécy and elsewhere. The Order of the Garter has remained as one of the most honoured and prized of all orders, although its scope has long since extended beyond the military field, and prominent figures in politics and the aristocracy have for generations been among its members.

By the sixteenth century many new orders had been founded, among them several which have survived until today. These include the Portuguese Order of the Tower and Sword, instituted in 1459, the Danish Order of the Elephant, dating from 1464, the Order of the Golden Fleece, 1430 (originally the order of the ducal House of Burgundy, but later regarded as the senior Spanish and Austrian order), and the Papal Order of the Golden Spur, for which the date of its institution is not known, but it was certainly being awarded in 1539.

The organization of orders varies considerably. Some, mainly the more important ones, have a King of Arms and a

Badges of ancient Orders: (*Top left*) Christ; (*Top right*) The Garter; (*Centre left*) Aviz; (*Bottom left*) The Golden Fleece; (*Below right*) The Elephant

Chancery or governing council, with a number of officials such as a Dean or Prelate, a Registrar or Secretary, and a Genealogist. Others are under the control of a central chancery or a state department.

Some of the very senior orders consist of one class only, but the most usual system is for the order to be divided into several classes, often three or five, but frequently with subdivisions. The highest class is usually known as Knight Grand Cross, with a large badge worn on a sash over the shoulder, the badge resting on the opposite hip; if the order has a collar, this is normally worn only on the most formal occasions, and then the Grand Cross badge is attached to it, the sash being dispensed with; in addition there is usually a

Two heralds — German (*left*) and Swedish (*right*)

The Dutch Military Order of William: (*Centre, above and below*) Grand Cross badge and star; (*Left*) Officer's badge; (*Right*) Knight's badge.

breast star, originally embroidered but nowadays of silver-gilt, silver, and enamel. The next class is usually that of Commander, but this may be in two grades, the higher of which may be called Grand Officer; they wear a neck badge, and the higher (or both) may also have a breast star. The lowest classes are usually termed Officer and Knight, Chevalier, or Member, who wear the badge on the left breast with other decorations and medals, the Officer grade frequently having a rosette on the ribbon.

In certain cases, where non-Christians are frequently among the recipients, the term *Cross* is avoided, and the highest class may be called the Grand Cordon, or just the First Class.

Many orders which can be awarded for either military or civil merit have an embellishment when won in action, usually in the form of crossed swords between the arms of the cross, or on the ring above it.

THE ORIGINS OF DECORATIONS

Ranking below orders and above medals is a series of awards known as decorations, which include awards for gallantry and meritous service. While some are of old foundation, the majority date from the early or mid-19th century, or later.

From the earliest times personal awards have been made to those who distinguished themselves, particularly for acts of gallantry, or for successful enterprises in war. The Romans gave a laurel wreath or a civic crown, while in later times individual medallions were struck, often in gold, to be worn on a chain, as tokens of such services. Many of these decorations were unique, specially made for a particular service, but in time a number of similar pieces were struck as a standard pattern of award.

Medallions were struck for the defeat of the Spanish Armada; Charles I gave decorations for the 'Forlorn Hope' attacks in the Civil War, while the Commonwealth awarded several for victories at sea against the Dutch. But decorations and medals, as we know them today, did not exist until the Napoleonic wars.

After nearly two years of minor actions at sea, there was great rejoicing after Admiral Earl Howe's defeat of the French fleet on the 'Glorious First of June', 1794. Large and small gold medals were struck, the former for admirals and the latter for captains. A few of these were given with a gold chain for suspension, but the majority were worn from a ribbon, the large medals round the neck and the small from a buttonhole. For seventeen further actions, up to 1815, these gold medals were given to senior officers, while in 1810 the Army Gold Medals and Gold Cross were instituted for similar achievements. While naval officers could receive more than one medal, in the army a bar was added to the medal for a further award, and on the fourth occasion the Army Gold Cross was given, with the four battles inscribed on the four arms of the cross, while again bars were added subsequently.

(*Centre*) Gold medal of Elizabeth I ; (*Bottom*) Naval Gold Medal, 1794 ; (*Top left*) Army Gold Medal ; (*Top right*) Army Gold Cross.

Modern Decorations

From the personal awards of yesteryear, the system of instituting decorations ranking below the insignia of orders has spread to all countries. In the main they consist of badges – crosses, medals, and a variety of other shapes – worn either at the neck or on the breast with other medals. Although they are usually of gold or silver, bronze is by no means uncommon; the highest awards are not always those of the highest intrinsic value, as shown by the Victoria Cross, of which it is said that the ribbon costs more than the value of the bronze of the cross.

Among British awards, some decorations are given for gallantry in action, such as the Distinguished Service Cross (navy), the Military Cross (army), and the Distinguished Flying Cross (RAF), but others are for specially meritorious service, such as the Royal Red Cross (for women only) and the Kaisar-I-Hind Medal.

Decorations of foreign countries include well-known items, such as the Prussian Iron Cross, which was essentially a military award, instituted three times, in 1813, 1870, and 1914, and discontinued after each of the wars concerned; the French *Croix de Guerre,* dating from 1915; the Italian *Croce di Guerra*; the Dutch Bronze Lion; the US Medal of Honor, and the Polish Cross of Valour; these were, or are, all awarded for gallantry. Many countries have decorations for long or meritorious service for officers (those for 'other ranks' are usually classed as medals).

Also coming into this category are decorations for civil merit, including arts and science, education, hospital and medical services, exploration, and sport. The French *Ordre des Palmes Académiques,* awarded for valuable services to universities and scientific work, was, prior to 1955, a decoration and is still often referred to by its old title, *Les Palmes Universitaires.*

(*Above left*) Italian War Cross ; (*Above centre*) French Croix de Guerre ; (*Above right*) Prussian Iron Cross ; (*Below left*) Dutch Bronze Lion ; (*Below centre*) French Médaille Militaire ; (*Below right*) Victoria Cross.

BRITISH ORDERS AND DECORATIONS

The Most Noble Order of the Garter

For over six centuries the Order of the Garter – the senior of our three Great Orders – has been among the most highly respected in the world. And yet, despite extensive research, the exact date and circumstances of its foundation have never been proved beyond all doubt. It is however generally accepted that the Order was founded in 1348, by King Edward III, as a Noble Fraternity of the sovereign and twenty-five knights, consisting of his sons and 'the bravest in the land'. Although historians do not admit the story of the Countess of Salisbury losing a garter, which the king picked up and bound round his own leg, saying '*Honi soit qui mal y pense*', it could well be true.

The insignia of the order consists of the collar with the 'George' (introduced by King Henry VII), the garter itself, worn on the left leg, the star, and the sash or riband from which hangs the 'Lesser George'. Over the centuries the precise design of the jewels has changed slightly, but has remained basically the same. The riband originated in 1519, when Henry VIII allowed knights to wear a small gold badge from a thin gold chain or a blue neck ribbon; Charles II changed this to a sash riband of sky blue – a colour which continued with the Stuarts, including those awarded by the Old Pretender. George I changed the colour to dark blue, while in 1950 George VI approved the present shade of king-fisher blue, which is specified by a sealed pattern. Unlike most British orders, the Garter sash is worn over the *left* shoulder, with the badge on the right hip.

On ceremonial occasions the knights-companions wear a mantle of dark blue velvet, lined with white taffeta, with the star embroidered on the left side, a hood of crimson velvet, a black velvet hat with a plume of white ostrich feathers, and, of course, the garter itself. On such occasions the collar and 'George' are worn and not the riband and 'Lesser George'.

A Garter Star, Riband, and Lesser George shown with a Knight-Companion of the Order of the Garter.

The Most Ancient & Most Noble Order of the Thistle

The Order of the Thistle, particularly associated with Scotland and junior only to the Garter, dates in its modern form from May 1687, when King James VII of Scotland (James II of England) virtually founded the order, though he emphasized that it was a revival of a very ancient brotherhood dating back to the late eighth or early ninth century.

While this cannot be fully substantiated, there is no doubt that some kind of order existed, probably from the fourteenth century and possibly earlier, connected with St Andrew. The thistle appears to have been adopted as the national badge in the fifteenth century, and soon after was associated with the insignia of the order.

The mantle is a rich deep green velvet, with the badge embroidered on the left side; the collar, in gold and enamel, has alternate links of thistles and springs of rue, with the badge showing St Andrew, in green mantle and purple surcoat, holding his cross, with a surrounding background of gold rays. Some examples show a clean-shaven saint, but the more usual type is bearded. The sash riband, originally purple, but dark green since Queen Anne's revised statutes of 1703, is worn, like that of the Garter, over the left shoulder on occasions when the collar is not worn.

The Most Illustrious Order of St Patrick

The third, and junior, of the Great Orders – that of St Patrick – was, of course, associated with Ireland. It was founded in 1783, by George III, and was maintained up to 1922, when the last appointment was made; since then the membership has been decreasing with deaths until the last remaining knights are the royal brothers, the Dukes of Windsor and Gloucester.

The badge of the order incorporates the so-called St Patrick's Cross, but this is actually the red saltire of the FitzGerald family, adopted to represent Ireland in the Union Flag of 1801. The pale blue sash, unwatered (like those of most British orders), is worn over the right shoulder.

While the badge is usually oval, circular examples are known, also plain gold ones, pierced and engraved.

(*Above*) Badge and Star
of the Order of St Patrick.
(*Right*) a Knight of the
Order of the Thistle.

17

The Most Honourable Order of the Bath

As far back as the eleventh century the ceremony of conferring a knighthood included the taking of a bath, to symbolize the cleansing of the mind as well as the body. In 1399 it is recorded that Henry IV, at his coronation, was attended by Knights of the Bath, and it is accepted by some historians that the Order was founded at that time.

A badge, not unlike the basis of the present design, is recorded in 1605, and some twenty years later a red ribbon for suspension round the neck was authorized. Later this became a red sash, following the practice of the Order of the Garter, but worn over the right shoulder.

In late Stuart times the order withered, and was re-organized in 1725 by George I, as a reward for outstanding services to the country and, perhaps, as a 'stepping stone' to the Garter. There was only one class, Knight of the Bath (KB), and the badge was similar to the modern Civil GCB. The star was embroidered (metal stars were not generally issued until about 1860), and worn on the left side of the uniform coat or, in larger size, of the mantle, while on ceremonial days the badge was worn from the gold and enamel collar.

Early in 1815, at the end of the Peninsular War, it was necessary to make a large number of military and naval awards, and the order was accordingly enlarged into three classes, namely Knights Grand Cross (GCB), Knights Commanders (KCB), and Companions (CB). This was a military order, but retaining a Civil GCB with the old badge, and the insignia was as today (except that until June 1917 the CB was worn on the left breast). In 1847 the civil division was extended to include the same classes as the military division.

From June 1917 the Companion's badge has been worn at the neck, but previously, when worn on the breast, it had a gold or silver-gilt pronged buckle on the ribbon.

The chapel of the order is the beautiful Henry VII's Chapel in Westminster Abbey, where the banners and stalls of the Knights Grand Cross can be seen, and where the Ceremony of Installation, revived in 1913, takes place from time to time.

The Order of the Bath : (*Top and left*) Star, Collar and Badge of Knight Grand Cross (Civil) ; (*Right and bottom*) Star and Badge of Knight Commander (Mil.).

The Order of Merit

In June 1902 Edward VII instituted an award which, although it carries no title or rank, is certainly one of the most highly esteemed of British decorations. The Order of Merit, which ranks immediately after the GCB, is limited to twenty-four ordinary members and is in the personal gift of the sovereign. It is given to those men and women (although there have been very few women recipients) who have given outstanding services in war or in peace, in the armed forces, in science and literature, in the arts, and in similar fields. Members of the armed forces receive the badge, which is worn at the neck, with crossed swords.

The Most Exalted Order of the Star of India

Shortly after the Indian Mutiny, Queen Victoria decided to found an order particularly applicable to India, to reward ruling Indian princes and also Britons who had given outstanding services to India. Thus in 1861 the Order of the Star of India was instituted, in three classes – Knights Grand Commanders (GCSI), Knights Commanders (KCSI), and Companions (CSI).

No appointments have been made since 1947, when India achieved independence.

The Most Distinguished Order of St Michael & St George

This attractive order was founded in 1818, to reward citizens of the Ionian Islands and Malta (which had recently come under British protection), and also British subjects who had rendered outstanding services in those islands. Fifty years later, after the Ionian Islands had been ceded to Greece, the scope of the order was extended, and it has become the usual award for services to the Commonwealth, particularly for diplomats and administrators.

The chapel of the order is in St Paul's Cathedral, where the banners of the Knights Grand Cross are lodged.

The Most Eminent Order of the Indian Empire

It became necessary to institute an order junior to the Star of India, and in 1866 Queen Victoria authorized the Order of the Indian Empire, in the same three classes. The ribbon is officially described as purple, but is actually a very dark blue. As with the Star of India, no awards have been made since 1947.

(*Opposite page: left*) Order of Merit. (*Opposite page: right*) Order of the Star of India.
(*Below left*) Order of St Michael & St George (reverse). (*Below right*) Order of the Indian Empire (first type).

Royal Victorian Order – Star of Knight Commander

The Royal Victorian Order

In April 1896 Queen Victoria decided to institute an order which would be entirely in her personal gift, free from the political control which largely governed other honours and awards. Thus the Royal Victorian Order has · always been awarded for outstanding personal services to the sovereign or the royal family.

The order consists of five classes, to which, since 1936, ladies have also been admissible – Knights and Dames Grand Cross (GCVO), Knights and Dames Commanders (KCVO and DCVO), Commanders (CVO), and Members of the 4th and 5th Classes (MVO).

During Victoria's reign awards were given somewhat sparsely, but Edward VII was more generous. Unfortunately he often forgot to notify the registrar of awards made on the spur of the moment, and consequently some of the records are a little inaccurate.

Unlike other British orders, the badges of the Royal Victorian Order are numbered on the reverse, with class initials for the higher classes (C-Commander; K-Knight

Commander: G-Knight Grand Cross) but some of the early grand crosses are unnumbered.

Foreigners can also be admitted as honorary members, and badges of the 4th and 5th Classes awarded to foreigners had, until 1958, a rosette on the ribbon of the 4th Class and a small bow on the 5th Class.

Attached to the order are the Royal Victorian Medals, in silver-gilt, silver, and bronze (but the last has not been awarded since the reign of George V). Recipients of more than one grade can wear them both, or all. From October 1951 medals awarded to foreigners have a white stripe in the centre of the ribbon.

The Order of the Companions of Honour

This highly esteemed award, dating from June 1917, has been described as 'a junior class of the Order of Merit'. It carries no title or rank, and is limited to sixty-five ordinary members who have rendered conspicuous service of national importance. These include men and women prominent in literature, science, and the arts, as well as a few politicians and Commonwealth leaders.

(*Left*) MVO 5th Class. (*Right*) Badge of a Companion of Honour.

23

The Most Excellent Order of the British Empire

The Great War, 1914–18, was the first conflict in which a large proportion of the civilian population, men and women, were engaged in work of national importance, in industry, war production, and social services. To reward outstanding efforts in these fields it was necessary to institute a new order, and thus, in June 1917, King George V founded the Order of the British Empire.

There are five classes, as with many foreign orders, which comprise Knights and Dames Grand Cross (GBE), Knights and Dames Commanders (KBE and DBE), Commanders (CBE), Officers (OBE) and Members (MBE).

The original ribbon was plain purple, but when a Military Division was added in 1918, this was distinguished by the addition of a narrow red central stripe; unlike the Order of the Bath, no distinction was made in the design of the badges and stars. The original insignia showed Britannia on the central medallion, seated, but in 1937 this was changed to the effigies of George V and Queen Mary, while the ribbon was altered to rose pink with narrow pearl grey edges, and a central grey stripe for the Military Division (except for military Dames Grand Cross, whose $2\frac{1}{4}$-inch sash is the same as that of the Civil Division).

Recipients of insignia of the original design can continue to wear them with the purple ribbon if they wish.

Attached to the Order is the British Empire Medal, which is widely awarded to persons who are not eligible for appointment to the order itself. From 1922 to 1940 there were two types of the medal, the Medal of the Order of the British Empire for Gallantry (usually called the Empire Gallantry Medal) and the Medal of the Order of the British Empire for Meritorious Service. With the introduction of the George Cross in 1940, the EGM was discontinued, and the remaining medal was re-named the British Empire Medal (BEM). Since 1957, awards of the Order and the Medal, if for gallantry, have been distinguished by crossed silver oak leaves on the ribbon.

Order of the British Empire: (*Top*) Badge and Sash of Civil GBE ; (*Centre right*) Medal of the Order – BEM (Civil) ; (*Centre left*) Star of KBE : (*Bottom left*) OBE (Mil.) : (*Bottom right*) Star of GBE.

25

The Victoria Cross

Founded in 1856, during the Crimean War, the Victoria Cross has become recognized as the highest British award for valour, and takes precedence over all British orders and decorations.

Since its institution less than 1400 have been awarded, a very large proportion of which have found their way into regimental and naval museums, where they are an honoured and perpetual memorial to the gallantry of the men to whom they were awarded.

The George Cross

Second only to the Victoria Cross in precedence, the George Cross was instituted in 1940, for outstanding gallantry by civilians and also for service personnel for similar actions which fall outside the scope of military awards.

Sergeant O'Leary VC attacks the German machine-gun crew. ·

(*Above*) Imperial
Service Order. (*Left*)
DSO (Victorian).
(*Right*) George Cross.

The George Cross replaced the Empire Gallantry Medal, and holders of the latter could exchange their medal for the new decoration.

Perhaps the most famous of its recipients is the island of Malta, which was awarded the George Cross in recognition of the valour of its people during the Second World War.

The Distinguished Service Order

Ranking as an Order of Distinction (as opposed to an order of knighthood), the DSO was founded in 1886 to reward officers for meritorious and distinguished service in war. The badge was originally in gold, enamelled, but was changed to silver-gilt in 1887. The top brooch is an essential part of the insignia.

The Imperial Service Order

Edward VII instituted this Order of Distinction in 1902, for the administrative and clerical branches of the Civil Service at home and overseas. When awarded to women a silver wreath of laurel replaces the star as a background for the central medallion.

British Decorations

The senior decoration, the Royal Red Cross, instituted in 1883, is for ladies in the nursing services and similar work.

The Distinguished Service Cross dates virtually from 1901, when Edward VII created the Conspicuous Service Cross for naval officers, the name being changed in 1914. The equivalent army award is the Military Cross, instituted in December 1914.

With the development of air power in the Great War, 1914–18, and the formation of the Royal Air Force, it was necessary to provide suitable decorations and medals for gallantry in this new branch of the service. The Distinguished Flying Cross was instituted in June 1918, for officers and warrant officers, for 'an act or acts of valour, courage, or devotion to duty, performed whilst flying in active operations against the enemy'.

The Air Force Cross is a similar type of award, but the wording here is '. . . whilst flying, though not in active operations against the enemy'.

Both crosses are of unusual design, and originally had ribbons with horizontal stripes of violet and white, and red and white respectively. These were changed a year later to the present diagonally striped ribbons.

The equivalent awards for non-commissioned officers and other ranks are the Distinguished Flying Medal and the Air Force Medal, with ribbons of the same colours as the respective crosses but with much narrower stripes; they too, originally had ribbons with horizontal stripes.

Second and subsequent awards of all four of these insignia are marked by a distinctive bar bearing the RAF eagle, with outstretched wings.

As with most other decorations, neither the DFC nor the AFC is issued named, but since 1939 the year of award is engraved on the reverse of the lower limb of the cross. The medals are named on issue, but any named crosses have been privately engraved, for recipients or their relatives.

(*Top left*) Air Force Cross ; (*Top right*) Distinguished Flying Cross ; (*Centre*) Distinguished Service Cross : (*Bottom left*) Military Cross ; (*Bottom right*) Royal Red Cross.

The Order of St John of Jerusalem

'The Order of St John' is the official short title of the Grand Priory in the British Realm of the Most Venerable Order of the Hospital of St John of Jerusalem, as set out in the Royal Charter of 15 March 1955.

The order is, of course, extremely old in origin, but is quite unlike other British orders. Descended from the Crusading Knights of St John, the British branch of the modern order was granted a charter in 1888, and is still mainly associated with hospital work, first aid, and social services.

Although completely separate from branches in other countries, including the Sovereign Order of Malta, there is a great similarity in the insignia, with the white Maltese cross as the basis. The British insignia has, in most cases, lions and unicorns in the angles of the cross, as the distinguishing mark.

There are five main classes, whose insignia is worn in the same way as other orders: Bailiffs and Dames Grand Cross, who wear their badges from a sash; Knights and Dames, of Justice or of Grace; Commanders; Officers; and Serving Brothers and Sisters. Male members of the second and third classes wear a neck badge, while those of the fourth and fifth classes wear their badges on the left breast with other decorations and medals. Women members of all four classes wear the badge on a ribbon bow, except when in uniform, when they wear them in the same manner as men.

All these badges are worn with a plain black ribbon (the width varying according to the class), but Associates have a narrow white central stripe; very broadly, they are either British or Commonwealth subjects who are not of the Christian faith, or foreigners.

In addition to these insignia, there is also a Service Medal and a Life Saving Medal, while those who served in the South African War, 1899–1902, and those who assisted with the despatch of stores and medical comforts, were awarded the St John South African War Medal.

(*Opposite page*)
Badges of a Knight (*left*) and a Serving Brother (*right*)

A Bailiff Grand Cross and his personal banner

FOREIGN ORDERS AND DECORATIONS

The majority of countries in the modern world, whether they be kingdoms or republics, have a system of orders and decorations similar to the British ones already described.

Some, as we have already seen, are of ancient origin, while others are so new that their statutes and insignia are still provisional. Few of the orders confer knighthood as we know it, yet many of them are regarded with the highest esteem, not only in their country of origin, but throughout the world.

From the collector's viewpoint, it is not always easy to know which are genuine examples of insignia, as in many cases there is no 'sealed pattern'. The badges and stars have been made over a period of many years, by various manufacturers in more than one country; but the largest problem lies in the fact that, unlike Britain, in many countries the recipients have to purchase their insignia. Consequently many jewellers carry stocks, in a range of qualities, to suit all pockets; and these can also be bought by collectors as well as by the recipients of the honours. Thus when an example

Arms of the Duke of Wellington encircled with the Garter and the Collar and Grand Cross of the Order of the Bath (Mil.)

appears in an auction sale or a dealer's list, one cannot always be sure whether it was actually worn by an entitled recipient or not. However, if the design is correct and the workmanship up to standard, then it is generally acceptable to most collectors. It should, of course, be remembered that over a long period of years there may well have been minor changes in a virtually unaltered design, while political changes may well occasion alterations or modifications – the French Legion of Honour is a good example of this, with the basic design being maintained, but with changes in the emblems of empires, kingdoms, and republics.

With many of the older orders and decorations it is not always possible to be certain of the precise shade of the ribbon; existing pieces of original or contemporary ribbon are usually faded, and in any case there is no doubt that in years gone by, the authorities were not always particular that ribbons were correct. Thus we find insignia with, say, narrow side stripes to the ribbon, while other examples have wide stripes, and the collector must not be too dogmatic on such points.

Grand Cordon

Grand Officer

Commander

Officer

Chevalier

Legion of Honour: ribbons with rosettes, etc., when ribbons only are worn.

EUROPE

The Order of the Golden Fleece

During the Middle Ages many rulers in Europe had instituted orders of chivalry, some of which are still existing today. Duke Philip the Good, head of the House of Burgundy, decided that he, too, should found such an order, the objects of which were to revere God and to protect the Christian religion.

Thus the Order of the Golden Fleece was instituted at his court in Bruges on 10 January 1430 (sometimes given as 1429, as the year changed in March).

In 1477, with the death of Charles the Bold, the control of the House of Burgundy passed to Archduke Maximilian of Austria, the first sovereign head of the House of Hapsburg. The Emperor Charles V, third head of the House, abdicated in 1565 and renounced his powers over the Netherlands and his sovereign rights in the Order, both of which passed to his son, Philip II of Spain. The seventh sovereign head, Charles II died in 1700, and left his Spanish lands to his nephew of the House of

Bourbon, while his Austrian possessions remained with the House of Hapsburg. Thus the Order of the Golden Fleece was divided into an Austrian and a Spanish branch, each of which has continued to make awards.

Like the Order of the Garter, there has always been only one class, but no breast star. Badges are sometimes found studded with precious stones, and these were given to specially favoured recipients. The Order was always very select – in the last 500 years averaging less than four a year. The Austrian branch has always restricted its members to Roman Catholics, but the Spanish branch has made a number of awards to Protestants and a few to non-Christians.

Many of the badges which appear for sale have been made for collectors and are thus not so desirable as those with a known provenance.

(*Left*) Philip the Good, Duke of Burgundy, founder of the Order, 1430.

(*Right above*) Spanish 18th-cent. jewelled badge.

(*Right below*) Austrian 19th-cent. badge.

Austria

The old Austrian Empire, which had grown out of the Holy Roman Empire, was understandably one of the countries in which orders of knighthood were of considerable military and social importance. We have already seen how the Order of the Golden Fleece became divided between Spain and Austria, but the senior award for war services was the Military Order of Maria Theresa, founded by the empress in 1757. The simple obverse inscription, FORTITUDINI (for bravery), surrounds the central medallion in the colours of the Austrian flag. This infrequently awarded order was in three classes, the Grand Cross of which was conferred on the Duke of Wellington.

The highest decoration for civilian merit was also founded by Maria Theresa, in 1764 – the Royal Hungarian Order of St Stephen – and similarly in three classes only. Above the cross is the old Hungarian royal crown of St Stephen, who founded the Hungarian monarchy in AD 997, and received the title of Apostolic King from the Pope.

(*Below right*) Archduke Charles of Austria, wearing the sash and star of the Maria Theresa Order. (*Below left*) Star of the Order of the Iron Crown.

(*Left*) Order of the Iron Crown. (*Right*) Order of Leopold.

The motto, INTEGRITATE ET MERITO (By integrity and merit) of the Imperial Order of Leopold aptly describes the purpose of this decoration, founded by Franz I in January 1808, in honour of his father, Leopold II. Gold laurel branches below the crown indicated an award for war services, while a peacetime award to a holder of a lower class with this *Kriegsdekoration* carried a laurel wreath between the arms of the cross. From 1916 the order was awarded 'with swords' when won in the face of the enemy.

In May 1805 Napoleon was crowned King of Italy, with the ancient iron crown of Lombardy, and the following month he instituted an order of that name. The crown consisted of a circlet ornamented with jewels, enclosing an iron ring alleged to have been fashioned from a nail from the True Cross. In 1816 the order was revived by Franz I, as the Imperial Austrian Order of the Iron Crown; the French eagle was replaced by the double-headed Austrian variety, and the ribbon now had blue edges in place of green. For war service awards laurel sprays were added at the sides. Genuine examples of the insignia have a hollow base to the crown-circlet, in which is a flattened iron ring.

One of the most powerful European military orders of knighthood was the Teutonic Order – *der Deutsche Ritter-Orden*. Starting as a religious hospital order in 1128, founded in Jerusalem for pilgrims to the Holy Sepulchre, the Brotherhood of the Sankt Marianer Hospital had various titles during the ensuing years, eventually becoming military in nature, and known as the Teutonic (or German) Order. Their foundation is usually put at 1190. After the fall of Acre in 1291, they turned to Europe, eventually establishing themselves in Prussia. In their white cloaks with a black cross on the left side, they were great fighters, gaining both power and lands, until their defeat at Tannenberg, in 1410, by the Poles. After that they declined in power, and by the nineteenth century had become virtually an order of distinction and merit. In 1929 however, the order reverted to its original form of a religious order of priests, lay brothers and sisters, and a number of honorary knights and dames.

(*Left*) The Teutonic Order. (*Right*) Military Cross of Merit.

(*Left*) Decn. for Science and Art. (*Right*) Decn. of Honour in Gold.

The Military Cross of Merit was instituted in 1849 as a decoration for officers. War services were indicated either by a laurel wreath or by crossed swords, or both.

After the 1914–18 war, republican Austria abolished the old imperial orders and instituted a new series of decorations. These, in turn, were completely revised after the Second World War.

The Decoration of Honour for Merit is the senior award (with associated Decorations of Merit and Medals of Merit) and is given for outstanding services to the republic. There are five classes, with sub-divisions of each except the 4th Class, the badges all being variations of a red Maltese cross with a thin white Greek cross superimposed, and the federal arms of Austria.

In 1955 the Decoration of Honour for Science and Art was instituted. Two lower grades of similar design constitute the Cross of Honour for Science and Art. The 1st Class is worn without ribbon, pinned on the left side, while the 2nd Class has a plain red ribbon and is worn on the left breast.

Belgium

The Kingdom of Belgium has only existed since 1830, when she broke away from the Netherlands. Since then she has created a highly esteemed system of orders and decorations, the senior of which, the Order of Leopold, was instituted just two years after the country gained its independence.

Originally in two divisions, military and civil (the former having crossed swords above the cross), in 1934 a maritime division was added, with crossed anchors in place of swords. The ribbon is officially described as *ponceau*, i.e. a poppy red, but actually it is a rich crimson-purple.

For awards for special merit during 1914–18 and 1940–5, the ribbons of this and other Belgian orders were embellished with either a central stripe or side stripes of gold thread. A few of these were woven, but it is more usual to find the gold stripes sewn on the normal ribbon. Furthermore Belgian orders and decorations often bear a variety of palm leaves, stars, crossed swords, and other emblems, to indicate various mentions in despatches and other distinctions.

In October 1951 it was decreed that except where inscriptions were in Latin, both wording and initials appearing on orders and decorations should be in French and Flemish.

Prior to 1908 the King of the Belgians was also the sovereign head of the Independent State of the Congo, and Leopold II had instituted several orders for that state. But in 1908 the Congo was annexed, becoming the Belgian Congo, and the orders were assimilated into the Belgian system.

The Order of the Crown was founded in 1897 as a Congolese order. In addition to the usual five classes, there is a sixth class of *Palmes* of the Order, in gold or silver, with the plain red-brown ribbon of the order differenced with white side stripes.

The other Congolese orders, now Belgian, were the Order of the African Star (1888), the Royal Order of the Lion (1891) – both for services to the Congo and African civilization – and the Order of Leopold II (1900), to reward services to the king.

(*Top*) Order of the Crown. (*Left*) Croix de Guerre, 1940. (*Bottom*) Order of Leopold (Maritime Division). (*Right*) Order of Leopold II, with palm.

For a small country, Belgium is rich in decorations, and one sees quite a large proportion of the population with narrow strips of ribbon on the lapel, from the buttonhole to the outer edge, representing anything from the Order of Leopold to the *Décoration Commémorative des Postes*.

In the order of precedence of wearing, the senior decoration is the *Décoration Militaire* (*article 4*). The Military Decoration dates from 1902, replacing a similar award instituted in 1873, and is also known as the *Médaille Militaire*. It can be awarded for long service, on a red ribbon with four yellow-black-yellow stripes (in which case it comes much lower in precedence), but under Article 4 of the regulations it can also be given for gallantry, on a red ribbon with black-yellow-red edges.

Immediately after the Military Decoration come the two *Croix de Guerre*, for 1914–18 and 1940–5. While both crosses were awarded for bravery in action, the earlier one was also given for long service at the front and other services. The two crosses are identical except for the royal cyphers, A and L respectively, while the red ribbons have, for 1914–18, five narrow green stripes, and for 1940–5, three green pin stripes on each side.

The two earliest Belgian decorations date from immediately after the breakaway from the Netherlands. The first was the *Etoile d'Honneur* (Star of Honour), instituted in 1831 as a mark of distinction for merit in the revolution for independence. There were three classes, two in gold and one in silver. In 1833 the Star of Honour was replaced by the *Croix de Fer* (Iron Cross), also awarded for service in the revolution, and also to those who were wounded. There was also the Iron Medal, virtually the second class of the Iron Cross, but it would seem that, although established by royal decree, it was only distributed as a souvenir or commemorative medallion; some, however, were fitted with a suspension ring and a ribbon, and appear to have been worn. The last survivor of the *Croix de Fer* died in 1904.

(*Above left*) Military Decoration (Article 4) ; (*Below left*) Ribbon of Military Decn. when given for long service ; (*Above right*) Star of Honour, 1831 ; (*Below right*) Iron Cross, 1833.

43

Bulgaria

Like other countries in south-east Europe, Bulgaria was conquered by the Turks, and from 1396 suffered under Ottoman rule until constituted an autonomous principality in 1878 (but still tributory to the Sultan). Independence came in 1908, as a kingdom, changing to a republic in 1946.

Prince Alexander I founded the Order of St Alexander in 1879, shortly after his election, for both military and civil personnel, for bravery and for distinguished services to the state. Military awards for war merit were distinguished by swords through the arms of the cross, while those given in peacetime had crossed swords on the ring. For special merit the first three of the five classes could be awarded with brilliants.

The National Order for Civil Merit was instituted in 1891, in five classes and a silver cross. The military division followed in 1900, with a very similar badge, but with the arms of the cross enamelled red; the oak sprays were replaced by crossed swords, and the ribbon was yellow with black and white edges.

Bulgarian National Order for Military Merit

Czechoslovakia: (*Left*) Order of the White Lion ; (*Right*) War Cross, 1918.

Czechoslovakia

The ancient kingdom of Bohemia – the land of the Czechs and 'Good King Wenceslas' – traces its history back to the end of the twelfth century. It was under Austrian rule from 1526 until 1918, when it was linked with Moravia, Slovakia, and Carpathian-Ruthenia to become Czechoslovakia.

The Order of the White Lion was founded in 1922, for award only to foreigners, in five classes, with the military division having crossed swords and the civil division crossed palms, on the wreath of lime leaves above the cross. The badge has been described as the most handsome of all modern orders. With the revised statutes of 1961, the order has been reorganized into three classes, and the design modified.

A separate and higher ranking order, but with the same ribbon, is the Military Order of the White Lion, founded in 1945. The design is somewhat similar, but with a normal four-armed cross. The War Cross, 1918, is of unusual design, the four conjoined circles showing the arms of the four states. It was awarded under similar conditions to those of the French Croix de Guerre.

King Waldemar's vision at Revel, 1219 (from a painting by
C. A. Lorentzen)

Denmark

The Danes have not always been the peace-loving people that
they are today, and their history as a kingdom covers some
1200 years or more. Denmark has only two orders, both of
ancient origin, and both highly esteemed throughout the
world.

The higher ranking is the Order of the Elephant (see page 6)
which in many respects has much in common with the Order
of the Garter. Its reputed date of foundation is 1464, but in its
present form it dates from the revised statutes of 1693. There
is only one class, and the membership of thirty is extremely
select.

Legend plays an important part in the story of orders, flags,
and heraldry, and is not always to be disbelieved. In 1219
King Waldemar II was fighting the pagan Livonians at Revel,
and at a critical moment he saw a white cross in the red sky,
which spurred him on to victory. It is believed that he adopted
this emblem as the flag of Denmark, the *Dannebrog* (which
remains to this day), and also the Order of Dannebrog. The
order was reconstituted in 1671 and enlarged in 1808, and
these three dates appear on the reverse of the badge.

Iceland

Proudly boasting the oldest parliament in Europe, Iceland was colonized by the Norwegians in the ninth century. Coming under Danish rule in 1351, she became a sovereign state under the Danish crown in 1918, and an independent republic in 1944.

The only order is the Order of the Falcon, instituted in 1921. The insignia was like the present design, but with a crown above the cross; with the revised republican statutes of 1944, the crown was replaced by a conventional lily. The falcon is the national bird of Iceland, and the ribbon reproduces the colours of the national flag, which is a rich blue with an offset cross of red edged with white.

The collar of the order consists of alternate medallions of the arms of the republic and the white falcon on a blue ground. The reverse of the original insignia bore the monogram of Christian X surrounded by the date of foundation, but in 1944 this was changed to just the date of the revised statutes.

(*Left*) Iceland : Star and badge of the Order of the Falcon. (*Right*) Denmark : Order of Dannebrog.

(*Above left*) Order of the White Rose (reverse) ; (*Below left*) Order of the Cross of Liberty (Civil) ; (*Above right*) Star of the Cross of Liberty (Mil.) ; (*Below right*) Order of the Lion.

Finland

After some 650 years as part of Sweden, Finland came under Russian rule in 1809, finally gaining her independence in 1917.

As a decoration for personal bravery and meritorious service in the War of Freedom, the Cross of Liberty was instituted in March 1918, but was replaced in 1919 by the Order of the White Rose. In December 1939 the Cross of Liberty was revived, and a year later became the Order of the Cross of Liberty and the highest military award.

The order has a grand cross and four classes, with two grades of the 1st class, the military division having two arms each holding a sword, on the wreath above the cross. The 3rd and 4th classes can be awarded with a Geneva cross in the centre, for medical services. Further, there is a Cross of Mourning for relatives of the fallen. The system of ribbons is complicated, but basically the military division has a red ribbon with narrow white stripes, while the civil division has yellow with narrow red stripes. Attached to the order are the Medal of Liberty and the Medal of Merit.

The Order of the White Rose is awarded mainly for civilian services, but can also be given for bravery in action, with swords; originally these were crossed, above the badge, but are now placed diagonally between the arms of the cross. There are five classes, from Commander Grand Cross down to Knight or Member. There is also a decoration known as Finland's Badge of the White Rose, awarded to ladies, and is a silver cross of the same design as the order, with only the central rose enamelled.

In 1942 it became necessary to institute a new order, to rank below the White Rose. Consequently the Order of the Lion was founded in five classes and a cross of merit. It is awarded for both civil and military merit, the latter having crossed swords. Associated with the order is the *Pro Finlandia* Medal, which is conferred on authors, artists, and scientists. The medal is of silver-gilt, and shows the Finnish lion as on the central medallion of the order but without enamel, and is suspended from the same crimson ribbon. The reverse bears the name of the holder, and the medal ranks after commander of the Order of the Lion.

France

Within the numerous orders of knighthood there is a small handful which stand out as the really great orders. Among these is the Order of the Holy Ghost – *l'Ordre du Saint Esprit* – founded by Henri III, the last of the House of Valois, in 1579 (some writers say 1578), and destined to be the senior order of France until the Revolution abolished all such royal institutions. However, the order, with others, was revived in 1814, until 1830 during the restoration of the monarchy.

There was virtually only one class, as with the Order of the Garter, but a number of officers of the order, some clerics and some laymen, were known as Commanders, and wore the badge at the neck instead of on the pale blue sash – *le Cordon Bleu*.

Knights of the order had to have attained the age of thirty-three, and had to be already admitted to the Order of St Michael (founded in 1469, but ranking below the Order of the Holy Ghost), and were consequently known as *Chevaliers des Ordres du Roy*.

In a different category was the Order of St Louis, founded by Louis XIV in 1693, purely as a reward for military merit.

The Legion of Honour

It is not surprising that one of the results of the French Revolution was the abolition of the orders of knighthood, but it was not long before even a republic based on *liberté, égalité, fraternité* felt the need for some kind of decoration to reward civil and military merit.

It was early in 1802 that Napoleon Bonaparte, First Consul, proposed the formation of a legion, a body of men, who had served France with honour. Thus the *Légion d'Honneur* originated in May 1802 as a brotherhood – the decoration came later.

On becoming emperor in 1804, one of Napoleon's first acts was to institute insignia in a form which has been maintained, with differences applicable to empires, monarchies, and republics, to the present day. These varieties of type, in their classes of Grand Cross, Grand Officer, Commander, Officer, and Chevalier, make a fascinating study for the collector who wants to specialize.

(*Above centre*) Order of the Holy Ghost ; (*Left*) Legion of Honour,
2nd Empire ; (*Right*) Reverse, 2nd Republic ; (*Below left*) Star,
Restoration period ; (*Right*) Commander's badge, 3rd Republic.

The National Order of Merit

Both before and after the Second World War, France had created a series of orders of merit for a dozen or more branches of social and industrial activities. The system had become unwieldy, and in December 1963 President de Gaulle united all these into the National Order of Merit, ranking below the Legion of Honour and in the same five classes.

The Order of the 'Palmes Académiques'

The unusual and attractive design of this order is nearly as old as the Legion of Honour, dating from 1808 as a decoration, *Les Palmes Universitaires*. It was originally awarded for services connected with universities, teaching, and for literary and scientific work. In 1955 the decoration became an order, with its present title. There are three classes; commanders, who wear a badge at the neck; officers, who wear a breast badge with a rosette on the ribbon; and chevaliers whose badge is of silver, enamelled, without rosette.

The Médaille Militaire

Prince Louis-Napoleon, President of the Second Republic, and later Emperor of the Second Empire, founded a Military

Star of the National Order of Merit

Medal – *La Médaille Militaire* – in 1852, as a reward for NCOs and men who had performed acts of gallantry or specially meritorious service, or who had been wounded in action. Later it was extended to generals and admirals who had specially distinguished themselves in war.

With the fall of the empire in 1870, the head of *La République* replaced that of Napoleon III, while the imperial eagle disappeared in favour of a trophy of arms.

The Croix de Guerre

First established in 1915 for officers and other ranks who had been mentioned in dispatches, and bearing various dates on the reverse for the 1914–18 period, the same design was authorized in 1939 for the Second World War. There was, however, a slightly altered ribbon, and the dates were amended.

In 1921 a variety was introduced for overseas service, with the reverse legend, *Théâtres d'Opérations Extérieurs,* and with a pale blue ribbon with wide red edges.

(*Left*) Order of the 'Palmes Académiques'. (*Right*) Croix de Guerre, 1914–18.

The Order of Agricultural Merit

An old established order which still remains is the *Ordre du Mérite Agricole,* dating from 1883. Like most of the lesser orders, it is in three classes: Commanders, who wear a neck badge; Officers, with a rosette on the ribbon of their breast badge; and chevaliers, who have no rosette and no wreath above the badge.

The Order of Maritime Merit

Another existing order, in the same three classes, is the *Ordre du Mérite Maritime,* but this is of more recent foundation, instituted in 1930. It is awarded to personnel of the merchant navy and to others whose work on behalf of shipping has proved worthy of recognition. The colours of the ribbon – blue and green – are symbolic of the sea, but the result is not as pleasing as it might be.

The Order of Arts & Letters

Among the most unusual designs of the modern French orders that of the badge of the *Ordre des Arts et des Lettres* is perhaps the most striking. The eight-armed cross, in dark green enamel, is quite unlike that of any other order. Founded in 1957 in three classes, it is given for outstanding services in the world of the arts and literature.

The Order of Liberation

Another unusual badge is the Liberation Cross, the insignia of the *Ordre de la Libération,* instituted in 1940 by General de Gaulle for both civilians and military personnel who had rendered signal services during the Second World War for the liberation of France. There is only one class, and the recipients are known as *Compagnons de la Libération*. Many resistance workers received it, some posthumously, and the nation's mourning for the fallen is indicated by the black edges and stripes in the ribbon. A large detachment of the *Compagnons* attended the funeral of General de Gaulle.

(*Above left*) Order of Maritime Merit; (*Centre*) Order of Arts & Letters; (*Above right*) Cross of the Liberation; (*Below left*) Médaille Militaire. 1870; (*Below right*) National Order of Merit.

Germany

Until 1870 Germany consisted of a number of separate states, of which Prussia was the dominant. All these were rich in orders and decorations, which have always been very popular with collectors.

Most of these states continued, under their own rulers, after the forming of the German Empire on 1 January 1871 (when the King of Prussia became the Emperor of Germany) until the abdication of the Kaiser in 1918.

There were no purely German orders (apart from the Order of Merit of the German Eagle, 1937, for foreigners only) until September 1939, when Hitler revived the Prussian Iron Cross decoration as a German Order.

Anhalt

The Duchy of Anhalt had only one order, the House Order of Albrecht the Bear, founded in 1836 and named after one of its illustrious rulers who flourished in the twelfth century. The insignia is of unusual design, being a pierced oval medallion; the ribbon is in the national colours – a distinctive rich deep green with wide red edges. In 1864 crossed swords were added above the badge when won in action against the enemy.

Baden

The Grand Duchy of Baden traces its ancestry back to Berthold, Duke of Zähringen, whose son, Hermann, was the first Margrave of Baden in the mid-eleventh century.

The House Order of Loyalty, founded in 1715, was very exclusive and was given only to sovereign princes, members of ruling families, and high dignitaries. There was only one class, virtually grand cross, but from 1803 to 1814 a commander class existed.

The senior military award was the Order of Karl Friedrich for Military Merit, dating from 1807, and there were two others which could be awarded with or without swords. These were the Order of Berthold I (1877) and the attractive Order of the Zähringen Lion (1812). The latter is a popular item with collectors, with its green glass arms to the cross, enamelled miniature of Zähringen Castle, and the ornamental scrollwork.

In 1916 the War Merit Cross was instituted, and was awarded to those who, in the forces or in voluntary service, had served with special merit.

(*Opposite page: left*) Anhalt : Order of Albrecht the Bear. (*Opposite page: right*) Baden : Order of Berthold I. (*Below left*) Baden : Order of the Zähringen Lion. (*Below right*) War Merit Cross, 1916.

Bavaria

Although Bavaria only became a kingdom in 1806, its status as a duchy goes back to the end of the ninth century. It was rich in orders and decorations, many of which include the national colours of light blue and white in the insignia or the ribbons.

The senior order was that of St Hubert, founded in 1444, to celebrate an outstanding victory gained on St Hubert's Day, 3 November of that year. There was only one class, with the badge worn either from a red sash with narrow green edges, or from a gold and enamelled chain, and with a breast star.

Older in origin was the Order of St George, reputed to have been founded during the Crusades and renewed in 1494 by the Emperor Maximilian I. Membership was restricted to the Roman Catholic aristocracy who had performed outstanding works of charity. The badge is unusual in that the obverse, depicting the Virgin Mary, is enamelled in blue and white, while the reverse, showing St George, is red and white. The

Knights of the Order of St George and the Order of St Hubert

(*Left*) Mil. Order of Max Joseph. (*Right*) Order of Ludwig.

ribbon is light blue with white side stripes, adjoining which, on the inside, is a narrow dark blue stripe, sometimes shown as violet.

The Military Order of Max Joseph dates from 1797. The classes were Grand Cross, Commander, and Knight, and were not awarded very frequently, as befits a senior order; less than 300 were given in the whole of the 1914–18 war. Just below this order came the Order of Military Merit, 1866, but much more widely awarded. The badge was a blue enamelled cross, with (except for the lowest class) rays in the angles. The central medallion bore the crowned initial, L (indicating Ludwig II, the founder), in a white garter inscribed MERENTI (For merit). When awarded for merit in action, crossed swords were added above the cross.

The Order of Ludwig, founded in 1827, is unusual in that it was purely a long service award. It was given, in a single class, for fifty years' service to the state, the court, the army, or the church, to officers or those of similar rank. Lower grades received the affiliated Ludwig Medal.

Hesse

When Philip the Magnanimous died in 1567, Hesse was divided into Hesse-Kassel and Hesse-Darmstadt, the former becoming an Electorate (*Kurfürstentum*) in 1803 but was annexed to Prussia in 1866, while the latter became a Grand Duchy.

Hesse-Kassel is perhaps best known for its Order of the Iron Helm, founded in 1814 by Elector Wilhelm I, as a reward for military merit in the war against the French.

The Order of Philip the Magnanimous, founded by the Grand Duke Ludwig II, of Hesse-Darmstadt, in 1840, was for both civil and military merit. It was junior to the Order of Ludwig, grade for grade, and eventually there were seven classes, viz. Grand Cross, Commander 1st and 2nd Class, Cross of Honour, Knight 1st and 2nd Class, and Silver Cross of Merit.

Like many orders of the German States, the motto of the order has a religious basis – *Si Deus nobiscum, quis contra nos*? (If God be with us, who can be against us?)

(*Above*) Hesse-Kassel: Order of the Iron Helm. (*Below*) Grand Duchy of Hesse: Order of Philip the Magnanimous.

(*Left*) Order of the Wendish Crown. (*Right*) Order of the Griffin (Mecklenburg).

Mecklenburg

The Grand Duchies of Mecklenburg-Schwerin and Mecklenburg-Strelitz shared the House Order of the Wendish Crown, founded jointly by the respective grand dukes in 1864. There were two grades of grand cross, grand commander, commander; and knight. The central medallion shows the crown of the Wends surrounded by a motto, which for Schwerin awards was *Per aspera ad astra* (By rough ways to the stars), while for Strelitz recipients it was *Avito viret honore* (He flourishes in hereditary honour).

Awards of the highest classes to ladies had the medallion set in diamonds, while military awards were distinguished by crossed swords. Another feature of this order was that although the ribbon was normally pale blue with narrow yellow and red edges, the grand cross sash was plain pale blue, but with an edge strip of yellow and red sewn on the ends, below the bow. Sashes are found, however, with normal edging throughout, and it is believed that these were used by foreign recipients.

Prussia

The highest Prussian award was the Order of the Black Eagle, in one class, founded in 1701 by Friedrich I. The orange ribbon was adopted in honour of his mother, a princess of the House of Orange. The order conferred heritable nobility, and, automatically, the grand cross of the Order of the Red Eagle.

This latter order, which originated in 1705 as the Order *de la Sincérité* of Brandenburg, became the Order of the Red Eagle in 1734. It is probably the most interesting of all the Prussian orders, with its many embellishments – with swords, both through the cross and on the ring, with crown, oakleaf, or bow on the ribbon, and with special designs for awards to non-Christians.

In 1667 the Order of Generosity was founded for military and civil merit. In 1740 Frederick the Great changed this into the Order *Pour le Mérite*, which in 1817 became a purely military award for gallantry in action. A separate division was created in 1842 – *Pour le Mérite* for Science and Art, with a quite different design but the same ribbon – and this is still awarded although very sparingly.

For 500 years the Hohenzollerns ruled Prussia, until the abdication of Wilhelm II in 1918, and in 1841 the Princely Order of Hohenzollern was instituted. In 1851 the Royal House Order of Hohenzollern was created, with insignia of similar design but incorporating the Prussian eagle.

Ranking equally with the Red Eagle but above the Royal Hohenzollern Order, the Royal Order of the Crown dated from 1861. Awards for medical services in wartime had a red cross on the upper arm of the badge, for the 3rd and 4th classes.

When these three orders were awarded 'with swords' for war merit, they were worn (except for grand cross or 1st class) with the 'war ribbon', i.e. a black ribbon with white side stripes instead of the statute ribbon.

(*Above left*) Order of the Crown (with swords) ; (*Right*) Order of the Red Eagle (with oak leaves) ; (*Centre*) Order of the Black Eagle ; (*Below left*) Order 'Pour le Mérite' ; (*Right*) Eagle of the Royal Hohenzollern Order.

Perhaps the best known of all foreign decorations is the Iron Cross, but it is not generally realized that until 1939 it was not a German decoration but a Prussian one. Also it was not a permanent award, but was instituted on three separate occasions and discontinued when each war was over.

The Iron Cross was first instituted in 1813, for the war against Napoleon. It consisted of a grand cross (sparingly awarded) worn at the neck, a first class and a second class. When awarded for bravery in the face of the enemy, the ribbon was black with white side stripes, and for other cases, white with black side stripes.

The second institution of the Iron Cross was in 1870, for the Franco-Prussian War. This Cross bore the date, 1870, on the obverse, while in 1895 surviving holders received an oak leaf cluster with the figures, 25, to celebrate the jubilee.

The last Prussian Iron Cross was introduced in 1914, with that date on the obverse; all three types had the foundation date, 1813, on the other side.

(*Left*) Grand Cross of the Iron Cross, 1870. (*Right*) Cross of the General Decoration of Honour, 1900.

Star of the Order of Louisa (for women)

The first General Decoration of Honour was instituted in 1814, in two classes, but in 1830 the 1st Class was incorporated into the Order of the Red Eagle as its 4th Class. After several changes the decoration was stabilized in 1900 as a silver cross with a gold centre, and a ribbon of the same design as that of the grand cross of the Red Eagle.

Prussia instituted several awards for women, including the Order of Louisa and the Cross of Merit for Women. The former was founded in 1814, named after the Queen of Prussia, to reward women who rendered outstanding services in war or in peacetime, particularly in the field of nursing. Originally in one class, in gold, with the dates 1813/1814 on the reverse, it was later enlarged into two, and finally three, classes, with dates 1848/1849, and later dates up to 1914.

The Cross of Merit for Women dates from 1871, on the suggestion of Queen Augusta, to reward merit in tending the wounded in the Franco-Prussian War, if the Order of Louisa was not suitable.

(*Left*) Military Order of St Henry. (*Right*) Order of Merit (with swords, for war services).

Saxony

Although the Kingdom of Saxony dated only from 1806, it already had a long history as a duchy and electorate for a thousand years. And before that, as a much feared warlike people, the Saxons had frequently attacked France and conquered Britain before they were completely subdued by Charlemagne.

Apart from the House Order of the Crown of Rue, the highest award was the Military Order of St Henry, founded in 1736 by King August III of Poland, Elector of Saxony. In addition to the four classes – grand cross, commanders 1st and 2nd class, and knight – there were also medals of merit in gold and silver. Kaiser Wilhelm II was awarded a special grand cross with a laurel wreath.

The Order of Merit was originally instituted in 1815 as the Civil Order of Merit, but in 1849 its scope was extended to cover distinguished military services, while from 1866 awards won in action were marked by the addition of crossed swords. The ribbon is in the national colours of green and white.

To commemorate Duke Albrecht the Bold, founder of the Albertine Line of the House of Saxony, the Order of Albrecht was instituted in 1850, for service to the state, including science and art. As with the Order of Merit, its scope was later extended to military merit, and crossed swords were added in such cases from 1866. The ribbon, in the national colours, is the reverse of that of the Order of Merit.

The badges of all three orders incorporate a conventional wreath of rue, the emblem of Saxony.

Meritorious voluntary services by women, in peace or war, were recognized by the award of the Order of Sidonie, dating from 1870, and named after the wife of Duke Albrecht the Bold. The badge bears a portrait of the duchess, and the attractive wide ribbon, violet with side stripes in the national colours, was normally worn as a bow, but could exceptionally be worn as a sash.

(*Left*) Order of Albrecht : Officer's Cross (with swords). (*Right*) Order of Sidonie (for women).

Württemberg

In 1805 Duke Friedrich (who had married the Princess Royal of England) took the title of king, thus establishing the Kingdom of Württemberg. But the country's history goes back some 700 years, first as a county and later as a duchy.

The senior order was the Order of the Crown, founded in 1818 by combining the earlier Royal Order of the Golden Eagle and the Order for Civil Merit. From 1870 awards won in battle carried crossed swords above the cross or behind the star, while in special cases the knight's cross could be awarded 'with crown'. The ribbon is described as carmine red (but for members of the royal house it was scarlet) with narrow black side stripes.

The Military Order of Merit, instituted in 1806, replaced the older Military Carls-Order, founded by Duke Carl Eugen in 1759. It was in three classes, but unlike most orders, the grand cross was worn at the neck, as was the commander's cross, but the former was distinguished by a large similar cross worn as a breast star. Up to 1818 the ribbon was yellow with black side stripes, but after that it was plain dark blue. Attached to the order were gold and silver Medals for Military Merit.

As a special mark of appreciation for meritorious service, military or civil, to the royal house and to the state, King Wilhelm I founded the Order of Friedrich in 1830, naming it after his father; it was in five classes, with two grades of commander and two of knight. Awards for merit in war were marked by crossed swords above the badge.

In June 1871 King Karl honoured his wife by giving her name to a new award, the Order of Olga. This was to reward men and women who had performed specially meritorious services in voluntary and charitable work, in war or peace, while in 1889 a lower award, the Karl-Olga Medal was instituted. The national colours of the country are shown in the black ribbon with red side stripes, and made up in a bow for awards to women.

(*Top*) Order of Friedrich ; (*Centre left*) Order of the Crown — Commander's star ; (*Centre right*) Karl-Olga Medal ; (*Bottom left*) Military Order of Merit ; (*Bottom right*) Order of the Crown (with swords on the ring).

Germany – The Third Reich

During the Weimar Republic, following the First World War, orders and decorations were abolished, but with the coming of the Third Reich certain earlier awards were permitted to be worn. However, it was not until May 1937 that the first order was instituted – the Order of Merit of the German Eagle – but this was only for award to foreigners.

With the outbreak of war in September 1939, the Iron Cross was again revived, but this time not as a Prussian decoration, but as a German order. The basic design was retained, but with the swastika and the date, 1939, on the obverse, while the ribbon kept the old Prussian black and white edges, but a red centre was substituted. Additional classes were added, including the Knight's Cross, worn at the neck, with embellishments of swords, oakleaf cluster, and brilliants. Recipients of the 1914 Iron Cross who received a 1939 award wore their old cross with a clasp bearing the German eagle, swastika, and the date, 1939.

The Order of the German Cross was established in 1941, in gold (gilt) or in silver, for exceptional deeds of bravery or leadership, and was worn like the star of an order, without ribbon.

One of the earliest decorations of the Third Reich was that for the Olympic Games, in Berlin, in 1936. There were two classes, the first worn at the neck and the second on the left breast, while a medal rewarded lesser meritorious efforts. Both the decoration and the medal were awarded to foreigners as well as to Germans who had given outstanding services in the organization of the games.

To encourage an increase in population, the Cross of Honour for the German Mother was instituted in 1938, in three classes. The 1st Class in 'gold' (bronze gilt) was for eight or more children; the 2nd Class in 'silver' (white metal) for six or seven; and the 3rd Class in bronze for five children. The cross was worn round the neck, from a long ribbon, 1 cm wide.

In 1945, after the fall of the Third Reich, all Nazi symbols were banned, but in 1957 certain decorations were permitted to be worn provided they bore no swastika or other Nazi emblem.

(*Top*) The German Cross;
(*Centre*) Knight's Cross of the
Iron Cross (with swords and
oak leaves); (*Left*) Olympic
Medal; (*Right*) War Merit
Cross (with swords);
(*Bottom*) Mothers' Cross.
(The Knight's Cross of the
Iron Cross, here shown
considerably reduced, is in
fact 48 mm wide).

(*Left and centre*) Badge and star of the Order of Merit ; (*Right*) Order 'Pour le Mérite' for Science & Art.

Federal German Republic (West Germany)

After the end of the Second World War all former awards of the Third Reich were abolished, and it was not until September 1951 that a new order was instituted – the Order of Merit of the Federal Republic of Germany. Founded as a means of recognizing services in the rebuilding of the country, and in other fields – social, cultural, and political – the order has eight classes, with three grades of grand cross, three of commander, and two of knight; also there is a medal of merit attached to the order.

The former Prussian order, *Pour le Mérite* for Science and Art, founded in 1842, was revived in 1952 after a lapse of some seventeen years, and is now awarded, on a restricted basis; the original design and ribbon have been retained.

In July 1957 permission was given for former German awards, such as the Iron Cross, the Cross for War Merit, the German Cross, etc., to be worn provided any symbols of the Third Reich – the swastika and the *Hoheitszeichen* – are removed.

Democratic German Republic (East Germany)

The decorations of East Germany follow the style of the Soviet Union in name, design, and method of wearing.

The Order of Karl Marx was founded in 1953, for distinguished services to science, culture, and the arts; like many Soviet awards, it can be given both individually and collectively. There is only one class, worn on the breast, with the ribbon made up in Russian style on a *kalodka* or pentagonal piece of brass.

For recognition of outstanding effort in productivity, the Order of the Banner of Labour can also be awarded individually or collectively. It was founded in 1954, also in a single class, and is probably unique in that two distinct ribbons are used for suspension, one being plain red and the other in the national colours of black, red, and gold. When the ribbon only is worn, this is red with a black, red, and gold centre stripe.

The republic has two other orders, each in three classes. These are the Order of Merit of the Fatherland (1954) and the Order of the Star of Friendship of Nations (1959).

(*Left and centre below*) Order of Karl Marx ; (*Right and centre above*) Order of the Banner of Labour.

(*Left*) Royal Order of the Redeemer. (*Right*) Royal Order of the Phoenix.

Greece

After four centuries of Turkish domination, Greece won its independence in 1829, following a war lasting eight years. And in July 1829 the Royal Order of the Redeemer was founded, in gratitude for the deliverance of the nation. Apart from a period of thirty years, 1833–63, the central medallion of the badge has borne an attractive miniature of Christ, and has always been a popular item with collectors. The usual four highest classes have the badge in gold (or silver-gilt), while the 5th Class is in silver.

The Order of the Phoenix was created by the Second Republic in 1926, but was awarded only to foreigners until the restoration of the monarchy in November 1935. Renamed the Royal Order of the Phoenix in January 1936, and with the crown added above the cross, it could now be awarded to both Greeks and others who rendered outstanding services to the country.

The original ribbon was watered, but from 1936 this was changed to an unwatered ribbon.

(*Left*) War Cross, 1917. (*Right*) War Cross, 1940.

Greece has a number of decorations, among them the War Cross, instituted in 1917 and awarded for bravery in action. Although bearing the dates, 1916–1917, on the reverse, it was also given in the Ukrainian campaign, 1920, and in the war against Turkey, 1919–22.

The decoration of the same name for the Second World War was quite different in design, being very similar to the French *Croix de Guerre* but with a crown above, and with a ribbon in three equal stripes, red-blue-red.

The Marine Medal was instituted in October 1925, as a decoration for those who had saved life at sea or who had rendered distinguished services to the merchant navy. There are two classes, the 1st Class being in gilt with a small gilt anchor on the ribbon, while the 2nd Class is in silver. One of the latter medals was awarded to a British seaman, who also received the bronze medal of the Liverpool Shipwreck & Humane Society, for helping to rescue the crew of a Greek ship off the Isle of Wight, in November 1930.

Italy

With the fall of the monarchy after the Second World War, the old Italian orders were abolished, including the very select Order of the Annunziata, dating from 1362, the Order of St Maurice & St Lazarus founded in 1434, and the Order of the Crown of Italy.

The Military Order of Savoy, however, which was founded in 1815 by Victor Emmanuel I, King of Sardinia, on his restoration, was allowed to continue under the title of the Military Order of Italy. There were slight changes in the design, but the original ribbon was retained.

The Order of the Crown has always been popular with collectors, with its delicate wreath of gold wire shaped into love knots. The obverse showed the Iron Crown of Lombardy (which also appears in the Austrian Order of the Iron Crown), while on the reverse was the shield of Savoy on the black Italian eagle. The order was founded in 1868 to commemorate the unity of Italy in 1861.

To reward meritorious service in the colonies, Victor

(*Left*) Military Order of Savoy, 1815 Grand Cross star. (*Right*) Military Order of Italy, 1956 : Commander's badge.

(*Left*) Croce di Guerra. (*Right*) Order of the Star of Italian Solidarity.

Emmanuel III founded, in 1914, the Colonial Order of the Star of Italy. Like the Order of the Crown it was in five classes, the four highest of which had a crown above the star. On the reverse was the legend, AL MERITO COLONIALE.

The design of the badge appears to have influenced the insignia of the modern Order of the Star of Italian Solidarity, founded in 1947. The badge is a five-pointed gilt star with an oval laurel wreath suspender, and is worn with a green ribbon with red and white edges – the reverse of the ribbon of the old Colonial Order of the Star.

In January 1918 the War Cross – *Croce di Guerra* – was instituted for acts of gallantry and meritorious service. Many were awarded to British soldiers and sailors in connection with actions on the Italian front and in the Adriatic and Mediterranean Seas. This issue bore the royal cypher, VE III, on the upper arm of the cross, with MERITO DI GVERRA on the central arms. In the modern version the royal cypher has been replaced by the monogram, RI (*Republica Italiana*).

(*Left*) Parma : Order of St Louis. (*Right*) Modena : Order of the Eagle of Este.

The Italian States

The orders of the old Italian States, prior to the formation of the kingdom of Italy, have always been popular with collectors, with their attractive designs and interesting history. Some continued to be awarded for many years after 1861.

The Order of the Eagle of Este, of the Duchy of **Modena**, dating from 1855, was awarded for civil and military merit until the death of the founder, Duke Francis V, in 1875. Military awards had a trophy of arms above the cross, while civil ones had a green oak wreath.

In the Duchy of **Parma** the Order of Constantine had a traditional history dating back to Constantine the Great, but of more recent foundation was the Order of St Louis, founded in Lucca in 1836 by Duke Charles, who later became Duke of Parma. In 1849 the order was taken over by Parma.

Lucca also had the Order of St George, for military merit, founded in 1833. The simple white enamelled cross, with the figure of St George on the medallion, was very similar to the badge of the Russian order of the same name (*q.v.*), but with a white ribbon with wide red edges.

The Grand Duchy of **Tuscany** had four orders, two of them dating from the sixteenth century. The Order of St Stephen was instituted in 1561 (some say 1554) by Cosmo de' Medici, re-constituted by Ferdinand III in 1817. The original object of the order, as a confraternity of knights, was to free the Mediterranean of pirates and to liberate Christian slaves from their Turkish masters. In modern times it was awarded for merit, and was in four classes. The Order of St Joseph, dating from 1514, was renewed in 1807 in three classes, but was very sparsely awarded, and was reserved solely for Catholics.

The Kingdom of **Naples,** or the **Two Sicilies,** was one of the most powerful of the Italian states, with a history going back to AD 1131. Of its various orders the best known is the Order of St Ferdinand and of Merit, dating from 1800. It was founded by King Ferdinand IV, to reward meritorious services in connection with his restoration to the throne. Lord Nelson received the grand cross, the embroidered star of which he was wearing when he was mortally wounded.

(*Left*) Tuscany : Order of St Stephen. (*Right*) Naples : Order of St Ferdinand and of Merit.

(*Top left*) Order of the Jugoslav
Star. (*Bottom left*) Order of the
Jugoslav Flag. (*Top right*) Serbia :
Order of the White Eagle. (*Centre
right*) Order of St Sava. (*Bottom
left*) Montenegro : Order of
Danilo.

Jugoslavia

Composed of Serbia, Croatia, Slovenia, Bosnia & Hercegovina, Macedonia, and Montenegro, it was in 1919 that Jugoslavia – the Land of the Southern Slavs – was created as a monarchy, becoming a republic in November 1945.

The Order of the Jugoslav Star, dating from 1954, is awarded for cultural, political, and scientific services. The design is an adaptation of the state arms in an interlaced ornamental border. It will be noticed that neither in this order nor in the Order of the Jugoslav Flag, is any form of cross used, probably because some 12% of the population are Moslems.

The Order of the Jugoslav Flag was founded in 1947, also revised in 1961, to reward distinguished services in furthering friendly relations between Jugoslavia and other countries. It is awarded in the usual five classes, the ribbon reproducing the colours of the flag, blue, white, and red, and for the two lowest classes, worn on the left breast, is made up in a form similar to Russian ribbons.

Serbia, Montenegro

The former kingdom of Serbia was restored in 1882, and in the following year King Milan I founded the Order of the White Eagle to commemorate this event. In five classes, the handsome badge of the double-headed white eagle bore a medallion with a white cross on a red ground, with four gold firesteels in the angles. Up to 1903 the reverse showed the cypher of Milan I, but from 1904 (following the assassination of his son, Alexander, and the return of the Karageorge dynasty), this was replaced by the date of the restoration of the kingdom, 1882.

The Order of St Sava was awarded for services to literature, arts, and science, but later was particularly associated with medical and hospital services.

As with all Serbian orders, a plain red ribbon was worn with both these orders when awarded for services in the First World War.

The Order of Danilo was established in the principality of Montenegro in 1852 to commemorate the gaining of independence, and was awarded for both military and civil merit.

(*Left above*) Latvia : Mil. Order of Lacplesis. (*Below*) Order of the
Three Stars. (*Right above and below*) Liechtenstein : Grand Cross and
Star of the Order of Merit.

Latvia

The end of the First World War saw the foundation of three Baltic republics, Latvia, Lithuania, and Estonia, which flourished independently until 1940, when they were annexed by the USSR.

Latvia instituted the Military Order of Lacplesis in November 1919, for bravery in the face of the enemy. There were three classes, with an unusual swastika cross. The central medallion shows Lacplesis, the legendary hero of Latvia, killing a bear.

The Order of the Three Stars was awarded for civil merit, and was founded in 1924, in five classes. The three stars, shown on the obverse, represent the three provinces, while the reverse is inscribed, LATVIJAS REPUBLIKA – 1918,G. 18 NOVEMBRIS, encircled by the motto of the order, PER ASPERA AD ASTRA (By rough ways to the stars). The pale blue ribbon has side stripes of gold thread. The order ranked immediately after the Military Order of Lacplesis, and both orders were inevitably abolished when the country was annexed by the USSR.

Liechtenstein

The tiny principality of Liechtenstein lies in the mountains between Austria and Switzerland. Nowadays its best known industries are tourism and postage stamps, but its history dates back to the Middle Ages. It was constituted as a principality in 1719, and from 1806 to 1866 it formed part of, first, the Rhine Confederation and, later, the German Confederation.

The Order of Merit was instituted by Prince Franz I in 1937, for award to both Liechtensteiners and foreigners for services to the state. There are five classes, but unlike most orders, there are virtually two grades of grand cross, wearing the badge on a sash – Grand Star, with a gold breast star, and Grand Cross, with a silver star – and two grades of commander, wearing a neck badge, but the higher grade wearing a small breast star. The badge of the fifth class is worn on the left breast. The ribbon, half royal blue, half red, reproduces the colours of the national flag.

Attached to the order are Medals of Merit, in two grades, gold and silver, using the same ribbon as the order.

Luxembourg

After the liberation of much of Europe from the Napoleonic yoke in 1815, the grand duchy of Luxembourg was annexed to the new kingdom of the Netherlands, the Dutch King William I becoming also Grand Duke of Luxembourg. His son, William II, instituted the Order of the Oak Crown in 1841, primarily as a merit award for Luxembourgers, but frequently given to his Dutch subjects as a junior order to the Netherlands Lion (q.v.). The badges of all classes except the lowest, chevalier, have a wreath of oak leaves between the arms of the cross. The order was lost to Holland in 1890, when Queen Wilhelmina succeeded her father, and thereafter is purely a Luxembourg award.

It is said that the colours of the ribbon represent the harmonious blending of the yellow of the broom and the green of the oak in the forests of l'Oesling.

The Civil and Military Order of Merit of Adolf of Nassau was originally founded in 1858 by Adolf, Duke of Nassau, for that duchy, but when Prussia annexed the duchy in 1860, the order fell into disuse. However, when the sovereignty of Luxembourg passed to the House of Nassau in 1890, on the death of William III, the new grand duke revived the order for Luxembourg.

There are the usual five classes, but these virtually become eight, as the grades of commander, officer, and chevalier can be awarded with or without the crown above the cross. The military division is indicated by crossed swords between the arms of the cross.

The Order of Merit was instituted in 1961, in five classes and a medal of the order.

The *Croix de Guerre,* created in 1940, is very similar in design to that of Belgium, and two types exist: the first, bearing the date, 1940, on the reverse, was awarded solely for the 1940–5 war period, but the decoration was revived in 1951, with an oak wreath on the reverse but no date. Both types have the same ribbon.

Among other decorations are the Military Medal (1945), the Cross of Honour and Military Merit (1951), and the Order of the Resistance, 1940–4 (1946); the last is a civil decoration, which has mainly been awarded posthumously.

(*Top left*) Cross of Merit of the Order of Adolf of Nassau. (*Centre*)
Commander of the Order of Adolf of Nassau. (*Right*) War Cross, 1940.
(*Bottom*) Star of the Order of the Oak Crown.

Order of the Netherlands Lion : Grand Cross badge (*left*) and star.

The Netherlands

With the end of the Napoleonic War, the Netherlands regained independence, and became a kingdom in March 1815. The following month King William I instituted the Military Order of William as a reward for gallantry in action and outstanding deeds of leadership. There are four classes – knight grand cross, commander, and knights 3rd and 4th class. The green diagonal cross of Burgundy and the firesteel in the centre are symbols of the Order of the Golden Fleece, which originated in the Southern Netherlands some four hundred years earlier. The insignia of the Military Order of William appear on page 9.

In September 1815 the king decided that an equivalent civil order was necessary, and created the Order of the Netherlands Lion, in three classes, for distinguished services to the country and to arts and science. The obverse of the badge bears the motto, VIRTUS NOBILITAT (Virtue ennobles), while the lion appears on the reverse.

These two orders are awarded very sparingly, and are consequently held in high esteem.

In 1841 the Grand Duke of Luxembourg, who was also the King of the Netherlands, founded the Order of the Oak Crown, and this was frequently awarded to Dutch subjects in cases where the Netherlands Lion was not suitable. But when William III died in 1890 and the young Queen Wilhelmina succeeded, this was no longer possible, as by Salic Law a woman could not rule in Luxembourg. Consequently in 1892 the Order of Oranje-Nassau was created as a reward for merit. When awarded in the military division, crossed swords appear between the arms of the cross, while the civil division has a laurel wreath. Medals of Honour in gold, silver, and bronze are attached to the order.

Not to be confused with the previous order is the House Order of Oranje. This is an award in the gift of the sovereign, founded in 1905, for distinguished services to the royal house, and rather similar to the Royal Victorian Order in Britain. In addition to the usual five classes, there are large Medals of Honour for arts and science, and also for initiative and ingenuity, Crosses of Merit in gold, silver, and bronze, a life-saving medal, and Medals of Merit attached to the order.

Prior to the Second World War there were very few Dutch

(*Left*) Order of Oranje-Nassau (Mil.) (*Right*) House Order of Oranje : Officer's badge.

decorations; Holland had remained neutral in 1914–18, and there had been little need for decorations outside the awards for gallantry for native troops who were not at one time awarded the Military Order of William. But being forced into war in 1940, both openly and 'underground', it was necessary to institute a number of decorations.

The senior of these is the Resistance Cross, instituted in 1946, in recognition of outstanding courage and leadership in resistance work during the occupation of the Netherlands. The obverse shows St George and the dragon, while the reverse has a flaming sword and broken handcuffs. It is a highly esteemed award, and when awarded posthumously it is given in a larger size than normal.

The Bronze Lion, created in 1944, replaced the earlier decoration known as the 'Honourable Mention', indicated by a gilt crown worn on the ribbon of the Expedition Cross or, later, on the Bronze Cross or the Airman's Cross. Subsequent awards of the Bronze Lion are indicated by metal figures, 2, 3, etc., on the ribbon.

Lower in rank than the Bronze Lion are the Bronze Cross (1940) and the Cross of Merit (1941). Further awards of both are also marked by metal figures on the ribbon.

The Airman's Cross, also instituted in 1941, rewards deeds of courage and initiative when flying in wartime. The ribbon, in diagonal stripes of orange and white, was obviously based on the British ribbons for the DFC and AFC.

Since 1869 the Decoration for Important Campaigns, generally known as the 'Expedition Cross', has virtually been used as a general service medal, with some thirty-three action bars, from BALI 1846 to TIMOR 1942 – nearly a century of minor actions, mainly in the former Dutch East Indies. The design of the medal was not changed when Queen Wilhelmina came to the throne, and was still used for the final issue, struck in Australia by the firm of Stokes, of Melbourne, for the bar, TIMOR 1942, awarded to the guerilla troops who fought against the Japanese on that island, and to members of the Royal Dutch Navy who transported them to Australia.

(*Top left*) Airman's Cross. (*Right*) Cross of Merit. (*Centre*) Resistance Cross. (*Bottom left*) Bronze Cross. (*Right*) Bronze Lion.

Norway

After four hundred years of union with Denmark, Norway was ceded to Sweden in 1814, becoming an independent kingdom only in 1905.

King Oscar I instituted the Order of St Olaf in 1847, to commemorate the liberation of the country in 1015 by the saint-king Olaf II. The classes are grand cross, commander with star, commander, and knights 1st and 2nd class; there is also a medal of the order. In each angle of the cross is the crowned initial, O, which is sometimes stated as indicating 'Olaf', but does in fact refer to the founder, Oscar I.

A collar or chain was introduced in 1882, but unlike British orders, where the insignia of a knight grand cross includes the collar, the grand cross of St Olaf is only occasionally awarded 'with chain'.

Crossed swords between the top of the cross and the crown mark military awards (including naval and air force).

It is interesting to note that the rampant lion (the arms of Norway) carries the battle-axe of King Olaf II.

Collar and Grand Cross of the Order of St Olaf

(*Left*) War Cross, 1941. (*Right*) King Haakon VII's Cross of Liberty.

When the Order of the Norwegian Lion was founded in 1904, by King Oscar II (Norway then still being united with Sweden), it was intended that this should be the senior Norwegian order, ranking with the Swedish Order of the Seraphim. But when Norway became independent in 1905, the order was abolished. Like the Seraphim, this order had only one class, but was unusual in that the badge was an oval medallion, while the eight-pointed star was so positioned that there were two points at the top, the bottom, and on each side.

During the Nazi occupation from 1940 to 1945, Norwegians still fought on, both in the resistance movement and in the exiled Free Norwegian Forces. King Haakon VII, himself in exile in Britain, instituted the War Cross in 1941 for Norwegians and foreigners who had shown outstanding bravery or leadership during the war. It is worn before all other decorations. With the liberation of Norway, King Haakon founded the Cross of Liberty for special merit and services to Norway. Both these decorations have affiliated medals.

Papal Orders

From the earliest days of orders of knighthood, from their development from the great religious orders, the Holy See, now usually called the Vatican State, has instituted and conferred a number of orders.

The Order of Pius, founded in 1847 by Pope Pius IX, recalls an earlier order of the same name instituted by Pius IV in 1559/60. Apart from the badge and star of the highest class, Grand Collar, which records the fact that Pius XII enlarged the order in 1957, the other insignia is inscribed, PIUS IX on the obverse, with the date of the modern foundation, 1847, on the reverse. It is awarded for personal services to the Pope and the Holy See.

Perhaps better known, and more frequently awarded, is the Order of St Gregory the Great, instituted by Pope Gregory XVI in 1831, and named after his illustrious seventh-century predecessor, Gregory I. The military division has a trophy of arms above the badge, while the civil division has a green laurel wreath.

(*Left*) Order of Pius. (*Right*) Order of St Gregory the Great.

(*Left*) Order of St Sylvester. (*Right*) Cross of Honour, 'Pro Ecclesia et Pontifice'.

The Order of St Sylvester dates from 1841, when Pope Gregory XVI revised the ancient Order of the Golden Spur, re-naming it after Pope Sylvester I who is alleged to have founded it in the fourth century. The true date of foundation is not known, but certainly the Golden Spur was being awarded in the mid-sixteenth century.

The badge showed its connection with the older order by having a golden spur attached to the points of the bottom arm of the cross, but when the Order of the Golden Spur was revived in its own right, in 1905, this appendage was removed from the St Sylvester badge and transferred to that of the Golden Spur.

There have been a number of papal decorations, the best known being the Cross *Pro Ecclesia et Pontifice*, for devoted services to the church and the Holy See. Founded in 1888 by Pope Leo XIII, whose bust appears on the central medallion, the cross, or its ribbon, can frequently be seen worn by Catholics of many countries.

(*Left*) Order of the White Eagle. (*Right*) Order of Polonia Restituta.

Poland

After more than 800 years as a powerful kingdom, suffering partition three times during the eighteenth century, Poland was ultimately declared a Russian province in the nineteenth century. She gained her independence, as a republic, in 1918, but suffered a further partition in 1939.

The Order of the White Eagle was instituted in 1713, by Augustus II, although legend places its foundation much earlier. After the third partition, in 1795, it fell into disuse but was revived in 1807, and became incorporated into the Russian orders in 1831. At this stage the design was altered and the original light blue ribbon was changed to dark blue. The order was again revived in 1921, in a single class with a light blue ribbon, and reverting to a design rather similar to the original Polish insignia.

The Order of Military Merit – *Virtuti Militari* – founded in 1792, has always been a most highly esteemed award. Discontinued soon after its foundation, it was revived in 1807, passed into Russian control, but became Polish again in 1919.

It is still awarded, in its five classes, under the Soviet dominated regime.

When the new Poland emerged after the First World War, the Order of Polonia Restituta – the restored Poland – was founded as an award for civil merit, in five classes, in 1921. The services for which it was, and is, given cover a wide field, from culture to agriculture. The original design had the year of Poland's liberation, 1918, on the reverse, but the order was renewed in 1944, with that year on the reverse and other slight changes. The ribbon is in the national colours of red and white.

For services in the First World War, the Cross of Valour was founded in 1920 and was renewed in 1944. The original issue had a purple ribbon with wide white side stripes, and these colours were reversed for awards in the Second World War.

In 1923 the Cross of Merit was instituted for both civil and military services, in three classes, gold, silver, and bronze, enamelled red for the two highest classes; it was renewed with modifications in 1944. The silver cross could, from 1928, also be awarded for bravery, so inscribed, and with a narrow strip of ribbon, half light blue, half green, sewn diagonally across the normal ribbon.

(*Left*) Order 'Virtuti Militari'. (*Centre*) Cross of Merit. (*Right*) War Cross, 1944

Portugal

With Spain, Portugal was one of the homes of the great religious military orders originating in the twelfth century. In comparatively modern times such of these orders as survived were, in the main, secularized into orders of knighthood or merit as we now know them. There is some doubt about the exact year of foundation of most of these early orders, and consequently some variations must be expected.

The Military Order of St Benedict of Aviz (generally known as the Order of Aviz) dates from about 1162 as a military body dedicated to fighting the Moors, but was secularized in 1789. Also of twelfth-century origin was the Military Order of St James of the Sword (or of Compostella). This was originally a Spanish order but a Portuguese branch was formed shortly after its foundation, also becoming secularized in 1789. The third and highest of the great Portuguese orders is the Order of Christ, which was virtually a revival, in 1317/9, of the then recently abolished Order of Knights Templar, dating from the early twelfth century. It was also awarded by the Pope, and the two branches have continued to exist.

These are the great orders, and for many centuries, when any two or all three have been awarded, a combined badge has been used, with a ribbon of the two or three colours.

The Order of the Tower and Sword, instituted in 1459 as the Order of the Sword, was revived in 1808 under its present title. A large number of British army and naval officers have received this award, both for the Peninsular War and for later services connected with Portugal.

The Order of Agricultural & Industrial Merit (which is really two separate orders) dates from 1893, while the present century has seen the creation of several new orders. In 1919, with a plain yellow ribbon, came the Order of Public Instruction, for the teaching profession; another modern award is the Order of Infante Dom Henrique (1960) for outstanding maritime services and discoveries, and commemorating Prince Henry the Navigator.

(*Top left*) Order of St James of the Sword. (*Top right*) Order of Aviz. (*Bottom left*) Order of Christ. (*Centre*) Order of the Tower & Sword. (*Bottom right*) Order of Public Instruction.

Russia – Imperial

The great czarist Russian Empire developed over a period approaching a thousand years, up to the time when the last Czar of Muscovy, Peter the Great, became Czar of All the Russias in 1721. The old Russian orders date mainly from the eighteenth century, and their beautiful insignia are always popular with collectors. Often the badges of the higher classes are embellished with diamonds and other precious stones, as marks of distinction for favoured recipients.

The enamelling on the central medallions is usually a superb example of the art of miniature painting, and the insignia are often executed in high carat gold.

The Order of St Andrew, founded in 1698 by Peter the Great, was the highest award, in one class only, and was very sparingly awarded; most of the recipients were members of the Russian or foreign royal families.

The Military Order of St George dates from 1769, and was awarded for bravery and outstanding war services. The two highest classes were normally awarded only to generals, and the Duke of Wellington received the grand cross in addition to the Order of St Andrew. Attached to the order is the Cross of St George, in gold or silver, similar in design to the order, but without enamel; this was awarded to many British soldiers and sailors in the First World War, for gallantry in action (most of whom served in France – not in Russia). The order was so highly regarded that even the USSR still uses its black and orange ribbon for a bravery award, the Order of Glory.

In 1735 the Order of St Anne was founded by Duke Charles Frederick of Schleswig-Holstein, but through a royal marriage was transferred to Russia in 1797. There were four classes, while from 1855 crossed swords were added for war services.

The Order of St Vladimir, instituted in 1782 by Catherine the Great, was originally an order for civil merit, including academic and charitable services, but later was extended to reward military merit, with the addition of crossed swords.

(*Top*) Order of St Vladimir. (*Centre*) Order of St Andrew. (*Bottom left*) Order of St George. (*Bottom right*) Order of St Anne.

Originally a Polish order dating from 1765, the Order of St Stanislas was absorbed into the Russian orders in 1831. It was named by the founder after his name saint and the patron saint of Poland. There were three classes, the second being awarded with or without the breast star. As with most of the Russian orders, war services were denoted by crossed swords, while various medals of the order were awarded to 'other ranks' for services not eligible for admission to the order itself.

Perhaps one of the most attractive of all the Russian orders was that of St Catherine, founded by Peter the Great in 1714. It was very sparingly awarded to ladies of the nobility, although at first some awards are believed to have been made to men. There were only two classes, the badges of which were adorned with diamonds, the first class, worn with a sash, having considerably more than the second class, which was worn on a bow. In February 1970, a magnificent diamond encrusted star of the order was sold at auction in London, for £2500.

(*Left*) Star of the Order of St Stanislas. (*Right*) Order of St Catherine.

(*Left*) Order of St Alexander Nevsky. (*Right*) Order of the White Eagle.

Away back in 1241, Alexander, son of the Grand Duke Jaroslav II, gained a great victory over the Danes by the River Neva. From this victory he gained the surname of Nevsky, and became a national saint. Nearly 500 years later, Peter the Great decided to found an order to commemorate this man, but died before he could do this. His widow, Catherine I, carried out his wishes, and in 1725 instituted the Order of St Alexander Nevsky. There was only one class, given for exceptional civil or (with swords) military merit, and it ranked second only to the Order of St Andrew.

Like the Order of St Stanislas, the Order of the White Eagle originated in Poland, but the date of foundation is somewhat uncertain; it is usually taken as 1713, but some say 1705. The order was absorbed by Russia in 1831. In only one class, it ranked third in precedence. The original Polish ribbon was light blue, but this was changed to very dark blue while the order was under Russian control.

Russia – USSR

When the czarist regime was overthrown in 1917, it was not surprising that all the old orders and decorations were abolished. However, even in a soviet state the need is recognized for decorations, and more than a dozen orders have been instituted, many of them for military merit, but others are for industrial, agricultural, scientific, and cultural merit.

The Order of Lenin, founded in 1930, is the highest civil award, and can be awarded both to individuals and collectively. There is only one class, and unlike most Soviet orders, it is worn from a ribbon.

The familiar phrase, 'Workers of the world, unite!' appears on the badge of the Order of the Red Banner, which is awarded in one class only, to officers and other ranks, and also to civilians, for bravery in action or outstanding leadership. Like the previous order, it is worn from a ribbon, whereas many Soviet orders are worn as breast plaques, with only a ribbon for use when the decorations are not worn.

Despite their annihilation of almost everything connected with the czarist regime, Russians still have some regard for certain relics of the past. The old Order of St Alexander Nevsky, for example, has been replaced by the modern Order of Alexander Nevsky, while the Order of Glory, founded in 1943, uses the ribbon of the old Order of St George. It is awarded to NCOs and men of the army, and to junior officers of the air force, for bravery or meritorious service in action.

For outstanding services of the highest importance, the title of 'Hero of the Soviet Union' is bestowed. Recipients are also awarded the Order of Lenin and the Gold Star Medal. The latter was instituted in 1939.

Among the other Soviet orders are the following, with their dates of creation: Red Banner of Labour (1928); Red Star (1930); Insignia of Honour (1935); Hammer & Sickle Gold Medal (1940); Suvorov (1942); Kutuzov (1942); Patriotic War (1942); Victory (1943); Bogdan Khmelnitsky (1943); Ushakov (1944); and Nakhimov (1944).

(*Above left*) Order of Lenin. (*Above right*) Order of Glory. (*Below left*) Order of the Red Banner. (*Below right*) Gold Star Medal.

103

Spain

Many of the old Spanish orders, several dating from the Middle Ages such as St James of the Sword, Alcantara, and Calatrava, were discontinued when the monarchy fell, but some of them were retained.

The Order of Charles III is still extant, and was founded in 1771. It was instituted for military and civil merit, and after the Peninsular War a number of British officers received it. It is also interesting to note that in 1847 the grand cross was conferred on St Ignatius Loyola who, some three hundred years earlier, had founded the Order of Jesuits.

Another order which has been retained is the Order of Isabella the Catholic. Founded in 1815 by Ferdinand VII, to commemorate his return to the Spanish throne, it was named after the Queen Isabella who sponsored Columbus in his voyages of discovery. Like the Order of Charles III, it has frequently been conferred on foreigners for services to Spain. There are the usual five classes, and the design of the insignia bears reference to the spirit of adventure; the badge, the star, and the collar show two columns representing the Pillars of Hercules, two globes indicating the old and the new worlds, under the Spanish crown, while the initials, F, Y, appear on the reverse and in the collar, for Ferdinand and Isabella.

The Military Order of St Ferdinand dates from 1811. Like several Spanish orders, the 1st Class was the lowest and the 5th Class was the grand cross, but it was unusual in that the 2nd, 4th, and 5th Classes were awarded for bravery, while the 1st and 3rd Classes were given for very distinguished service.

Ranking below the Order of St Ferdinand were the Order for Military Merit and the Order for Naval Merit, instituted in 1864 and 1866 respectively. These two orders still exist, and when given for war services are enamelled red, but white for peacetime awards. In modern times an equivalent Order for Aeronautical Merit has been established on similar lines.

In 1856 Isabella II founded the Order of Benevolence, for charitable works. This order has been retained, now with a grand cross added, and has four divisions, with separate ribbons according to the services rendered.

As an award for merit in the fields of literature, science,

(*Above*) Grand Cross and star of the Order of Charles III. (*Below left*) Order of Naval Merit. (*Below right*) Order of Benevolence.

and the arts, King Alfonso XIII instituted the Order of Alfonso XII in 1902, in honour of his father. The insignia is unusual, both in design and colouring. The order is not to be confused with the modern Order of Alfonso X, the Wise, which replaced the older order in 1939; this later order is named after a thirteenth-century king, and the insignia is quite different.

Also outstanding with its violent colouring, was the much older Maria-Louisa Order, dating from 1792 but renewed and amended by Queen Isabella II. It was awarded to ladies of nobility, in one class only, and was worn from a narrow sash or with the ribbon made up into a bow. The medallion of the badge carries the figure of St Ferdinand, while the reverse bears the initials of Queen Maria-Louisa.

During the Peninsular War, as battle after battle was fought and Spanish towns were liberated from Napoleonic rule, many decorations were issued to those who had distinguished themselves. These crosses of honour are mainly scarce and much sought after by collectors; most of them are of silver or gold,

(*Left*) Order of Maria-Louisa. (*Right*) Order of Alfonso X, the Wise.

(*Left*) Cross for Alcala de Henares, 1808. (*Right*) Cross for Portugal, 1808. (*Centre*) Order of the Yoke and Arrows.

enamelled, with 30 mm ribbons. The earliest action so commemorated was that at Alcala de Henares, in May 1808. The gold cross was authorized by Ferdinand VII in 1817, and the letters, Z M P, on the flag in the central medallion indicate sappers, miners, and pontoon men, who successfully defended the town. Spanish soldiers who were forced into Napoleon's army, but who deserted in Portugal and returned to fight against the French, were awarded the Cross for Portugal, 1808. These are but two examples from more than fifty such decorations.

Modern Spain has a number of orders, including some of the older ones which have been revised, and appropriate changes made to the design of the insignia. The best known of the more recent ones is the Order of the Yoke and Arrows, founded in 1937, with five classes, grand collar, grand cross, two grades of commander, and medal of the order; it is given for outstanding services to the state.

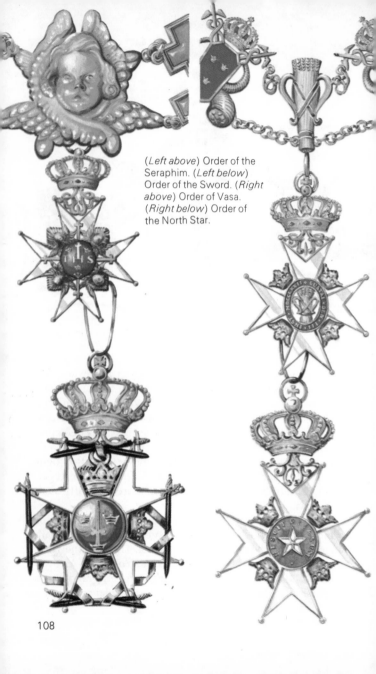

(*Left above*) Order of the Seraphim. (*Left below*) Order of the Sword. (*Right above*) Order of Vasa. (*Right below*) Order of the North Star.

Sweden

Although Sweden has a history as a kingdom since the eleventh century or earlier, it was not until King Gustavus I Vasa freed the country from the Danish yoke in 1521, that she became a real power in northern Europe.

The three senior Swedish orders all date from 1748, but have earlier antecedents. The Order of the Seraphim, the most senior, is alleged to have existed in the thirteenth or fourteenth century, but in its present form has only one class with a very limited membership. Outside the royal family, it is only awarded for the most distinguished services to the country, and recipients wear the badge either from a plain pale blue watered sash or from an ornate gold collar of blue patriarchal crosses and seraphim heads.

The Order of the Sword has, nowadays, five classes, and is awarded for military merit. Unlike most insignia, the arms of the eight-pointed cross are set diagonally, presenting an unusual appearance.

The civil equivalent of the Order of the Sword is the Order of the North (or Pole) Star, in three classes with two grades of the second class.

In 1772 King Gustav III instituted the Order of Vasa, named after his illustrious ancestor, Gustavus I Vasa, whose family ruled Sweden for nearly three hundred years. The order is virtually in five classes, there being two grades of both the second and third classes. It is given mainly for services to industry, the arts, agriculture, and public service.

The badge incorporates a wheatsheaf made up into the form of a golden vase, from the arms of Gustavus Vasa. Prior to 1860 it was in oval format, but now, reduced in size, this forms the central medallion of the white enamelled cross. Both this order and the Order of the North Star can be specially awarded 'with diamonds'.

Each Swedish order has its heralds who, like the Garter King of Arms, wear tabards of ancient design. One example, the herald of the Order of the North Star, is shown on page 8.

Sweden has few decorations apart from those associated with orders. Both the Order of the Sword and the Vasa Order have a badge and a medal, and the other two orders have medals; there is also the War Cross of the Order of the Sword.

ASIA

Among the many countries comprising the continent of Asia, only a few have orders designed on the same basis as those of Europe. Some countries, such as China, have had a system of complicated awards with some extremely picturesque insignia, while in other cases orders are alleged to have existed but information is scanty. Naturally where many non-Christian religions predominate, the insignia avoid designs based on a cross, but stars, crescents, and geometrical designs abound.

In our limited space it has only been possible to include a selection of the many orders which have existed; in the main,

(*Left*) Order of the Double Dragon – early type. (*Right*) Order of the Crystal Button.

Star of the Order of the Double
Dragon, 1911 type

these are the ones which collectors are most likely to en-
counter, and on which information is likely to be sought.

China

With the oldest monarchy in the world, dating back reputedly
to 2205 BC, China existed under the rule of emperors until a
republic was declared in 1912. Its complicated political
history is matched by its complicated system of orders.

The Order of the Double Dragon was instituted in 1881–2,
by the Emperor Kwang-Su. There were five classes, but each
class was sub-divided so that persons of different status were
eligible for different grades. Thus the three grades of the first
class were for heads of states, princes of ruling houses, and
hereditary noblemen respectively. Every class and grade had
its own colour ribbon, embroidered with pairs of dragons.

In 1911 the insignia was changed to a simpler design, the
badge being a star of five broad petal-like points.

An earlier decoration was the Order of the Crystal Button,
an award for military bravery instituted in the mid-nineteenth

century. On the reverse are four Chinese characters signifying, 'Bestowed by the great Emperor of the Tsing Dynasty'. The example shown was awarded to a soldier in the 67th (Hampshire) Regt.

The Order of Chia Ho, also known as the Excellent Crop or the Golden Grain, dates from 1923. Some nine classes are recorded, each with a distinctive ribbon. The following year, 1924, saw the institution of the Order of the Brilliant Jade, or Jasper. Again the nine classes all have different ribbons. The badge of the first class, illustrated with its red ribbon, edged white, has a centre of red jasper. The grand cordon had a plain red ribbon, while the second class reversed the colours of the first class ribbon – white with red edges.

The Order of Wen-hu, or the Striped Tiger, was created in 1912, also in nine classes. The ribbons of the classes are as follows: 1st class – red with orange edges; 2nd class – yellow with green edges; 3rd to 6th classes – green with red edges; 7th to 9th classes – white with red edges, and narrow blue side stripes; the ribbons are usually unwatered.

(*Top*) Order of Chia Ho. (*Bottom*) Order of the Striped Tiger.

Iran

The modern Iran derives from the ancient kingdom of Persia, whose origins are lost in antiquity. And with such a long history and culture, it is not surprising that the country has instituted a number of orders and decorations.

Best known perhaps is the Order of the Lion and Sun, founded in two classes in 1808 (as the Order of the Sun), but later extended to five classes. The design of the insignia has varied from time to time, and has been awarded to a number of British subjects.

In modern times the highest award is the Order of Pahlevi, awarded mainly to heads of states, but the Order of the Crown of Iran, also known as the Order of the Taj, is more widely awarded, in its five classes. The badge bears a resemblence to the French Legion of Honour, with its five V-ended arms and the wreath above. The first class has a magnificent collar, in gold and enamel, with ten miniature badges and twelve lions and suns. The ribbon of the order is also very attractive, being a rich medium blue with narrow white and green edges.

(*Below*) Badge and star of the
Order of the Crown of Iran.

Japan

Of all the major countries of Asia, Japan has the system of orders and decorations most closely resembling those of the western world. For over 2000 years Japan had developed her military power and history, rigidly excluding foreigners from the country until 1853. And with the opening up of communications and trade with Europe, Japan found the need to establish rewards for civil and military merit.

The Order of the Chrysanthemum, founded in 1877, is not only the most beautiful but is also the highest of the Japanese orders. In one class only, worn from a sash, it is rarely awarded except to members of the royal family and foreign royalties or heads of states. Like the Order of the Rising Sun, both the badge and the breast star have a large cabochon garnet in the centre. Four enamelled chrysanthemums are incorporated in the badge and the star, while the former hangs from a larger chrysanthemum.

The Order of the Rising Sun is two years older, dating from 1875, and is awarded for both military and civil merit. There are eight classes, the first six having a badge consisting of a star of thirty-two rays which, with the central garnet, characterizes the rising sun; the badge hangs from a spray of paulownia flowers and leaves. For the seventh and eighth classes the badge is just the flowers and leaves, enamelled violet and green for the seventh class, and in plain silver for the eighth class. The ribbon, white with red edges, reproduces the main colours of the badge which are also the national colours of Japan.

In 1888 a special senior grade of the Order of the Rising Sun was created, known as the Order of the Paulownia Sun. The sash ribbon is red, with a wide white stripe near each edge, while the badge is rather similar to those of the Rising Sun and the Chrysanthemum. It is awarded for exceptional merit, military or civil, and usually only to those of very high rank or station.

(*Top*) Grand Cordon of the Order of the Rising Sun. (*Left*) Supreme Order of the Chrysanthemum. (*Right*) Grand Cordon of the Order of the Rising Sun with Pawlonia Flowers. (*Bottom*) Order of the Rising Sun, 7th Class.

Instituted at the same time, but ranking lower, is the Order of the Sacred Treasure, also known as the Order of the Mirror. According to legend, the first emperor of Japan (*circa* 665 BC) left three treasures to his successor – a mirror, a collar, and a

(*Above left*) Order of the Sacred Treasure. (*Below left*) Order of the Golden Kite. (*Above right*) Order of the Crown (for women). (*Below right*) Cultural Decoration.

number of swords – and these are all conventionally represented in the badge of the Order of the Sacred Treasure; the mirror, in the centre, is surrounded by a collar of sixteen rubies (or red glass stones, according to class), while the rays represent the swords. The watered ribbon is a distinctive shade of light blue, somewhat greenish in hue, with a rich yellow stripe at each side, but some old badges have a very light greyish-brown ribbon with pale yellow side stripes; it is thought that these ribbons are merely faded, but they may possibly be a variety in use at one time, as supplies of new ribbon in these colours were available some years ago.

Another award for bravery in action was the Order of the Golden Kite. Legend says that *circa* 660 BC the first emperor of Japan was resting during a lull in battle when a golden bird, a kite or hawk, told him to change his plans and attack from the east; this he did and the monarchy was saved.

Many of the Japanese orders are, or were, awarded only to men; consequently in 1888 the emperor instituted an order of merit solely for women – the Order of the Crown – in eight classes. The ribbon is orange-yellow with narrow red side stripes, but some writers give it as identical with that of the Austrian Cross for Military Merit, white and red horizontal stripes with red and white edges. The badge is delightfully made, with a double row of pearls and clusters of pink and white cherry blossoms; it hangs from a suspender which varies with the class, the highest grade having a circlet of violet and green paulownia flowers and leaves, while other classes have such designs as white chrysanthemums, a butterfly, wistaria flowers, etc. The five-pointed star of the order is ornamented with over a hundred pearls, and also has clusters of cherry blossom; in the centre is the sacred ho-o bird, which also appears on the badge above the ancient crown of the Japanese empresses.

In modern times the Order of Culture, or Cultural Decoration, was founded in 1937 in a single class, as an award for Japanese men and women only, for exceptional services to the cultural life of Japan. The badge represents the five-petalled mandarin orange flower, and hangs from a cluster of the same leaves and fruit. It is worn at the neck from a pale violet ribbon.

(*Left*) Order of the Star of Nepal. (*Right*) Order of the Gurkha Right Hand.

Nepal

The kingdom of Nepal, famous as the home of the Gurkhas, has nine orders and ten decorations. The best known of these are The Order of the Star of Nepal and the Order of the Gurkha Right Hand.

The Order of the Star was instituted in 1918, and is awarded to army officers for meritorious service in the defence of the kingdom or in the maintenance of international peace. It can also be given to foreign officers attached to the Nepalese army.

In 1932 the Order of the Gurkha Right Hand was revived from its original foundation in 1896, to reward Nepalese for valuable services in any field of national life, and also to foreigners 'who cherish love and respect towards the Kingdom of Nepal'. The lower part of the badge shows two crossed kukris; the kukri is the famous fighting knife of the Gurkhas, and when it has been drawn from its sheath it must not be replaced without blood being drawn. Consequently if a Gurkha draws his kukri for peaceful use or to show it to a foreigner, he makes a tiny nick on his hand or arm before replacing it.

Thailand

Known as Siam until 1939, the kingdom of Thailand has a history dating back some six hundred years. It is also known as 'the land of the White Elephant' from the prominence given to this animal in legends, old flags, and emblems. The mother of Zacca, the founder of the nation, is supposed to have dreamed that she had borne a white elephant and this became the country's emblem.

The Order of the Crown dates from 1861, and is to reward civil and military merit. Rather similar in design is the Order of the White Elephant, also founded in 1861, as an award for national merit. Both orders have badges in typical oriental style, with a central medallion surrounded by rows of leaf-like ornaments, while the green-edged ribbons are also of rather similar design.

Another similar ribbon, but with a yellow centre, is used for the Holy Order of the Nine Gems, a religious order dating from the same period.

Order of the White Elephant:
(*Above*) Special Class usually awarded to heads of states;
(*Below*) First Class.

Turkey

When Napoleon's army occupied Egypt in 1800, it was obvious to Britain that his ultimate aim was India, and consequently a naval and military force was sent to oust the French. The Sultan of Turkey, under whose rule Egypt came, wished to reward the services of the British, and in 1801 he instituted a decoration known as the Order of the Crescent or the Sultan's Gold Medal for Egypt. It was given in three sizes, according to the rank of the recipient; examples in silver are known, but no information is available as to whom (if anyone) they were awarded. For almost fifty years this was the only medal which the recipients had to show for this action until, in 1850, the clasp, EGYPT, was authorized for the Military and Naval General Service Medals.

The Order of the Mejidie, created by Sultan Mejid in 1852, was frequently awarded to British officers, particularly after wars in which assistance had been given to Turkey, such as the Crimean War, 1854–6, and the Egyptian and Sudan campaigns of 1882–9 and 1896–1905. The red ribbon has green edges,

(*Above*) Order of Chastity.
(*Below*) Order of the Mejidie.

but often appears with the green slightly inset.

In 1862 Sultan Abdul Aziz instituted the Order of the Osmanieh, for meritorious services in peacetime, both for Turks and foreigners. Only the obverse of the badge was enamelled, the reverse showing a trophy of flags and arms in plain silver. Like the Order of the Mejidie, many British officers were among the recipients.

An unusual title for a decoration was the Order of Chastity – *Nichan-i-Chefakat* – reserved for ladies and founded by Sultan Abdul Hamid II in 1878. It was awarded for meritorious services in wartime and also in the field of science and literature. There were three classes, and one rather wonders if a lady felt any embarrassment when awarded the Order of Chastity, third class.

The Order of Merit – *Nichan-i-Imtiaz* – dating from 1879, had a corresponding decoration, the Imtiaz Medal, using the same ribbon of half green, half red. There was also another medal of merit, the Liakat Medal, using the Mejidie ribbon; both these could, from 1915, be awarded with crossed swords on the ribbon for war services.

(*Above*) Order of the Osmanieh. (*Below*) Sultan's Gold Medal, 1801.

AFRICA

Until quite recently Africa consisted mainly of colonies and other territories associated with a handful of European countries, with only a few independent sovereign states having orders and decorations. But in recent years many new countries have come into being, and although orders have been instituted by several of them, with so many changes in statutes and insignia, it has proved almost impossible to obtain authoritative information about many of them.

Egypt
After some 300 years of Turkish rule, followed by a period of association with Britain, Egypt became independent in 1922, as a kingdom, becoming a republic in 1953.

The Order of Mohammed Ali, instituted in 1915, was the highest award for civil and military merit, with a most attractive badge, delicately designed. The order was abolished in 1954.

The Order of the Nile, founded in the same year in five classes, was conferred on many British officers serving in Egypt. While the country was a kingdom a crown appeared above the badge and star, but as the order was retained when the monarchy was overthrown, this has now been removed.

Ethiopia
Legend takes the history of Ethiopia (or Abyssinia) back to King Solomon and the Queen of Sheba, but certainly the kingdom is of very ancient origin.

The senior award is the Order of Solomon's Seal, dating from 1874, and is only given for the most exceptional services.

More frequently awarded is the Order of the Star of Ethiopia, with its ribbon in the colours of the national flag, red, yellow, and green. It was founded in 1894, with five classes, and the design of the badge varies with the class; the two lowest classes have a peculiar design of a five-pointed star with the two bottom points joined and the space filled in with gold filigree work. Other Ethiopian awards include the Orders of the Queen of Sheba, Menelik II, and the Trinity.

(*Top left*) Ethiopia : Order of Solomon's Seal. (*Top right*) Order of the Star. (*Bottom left*) Egypt : Order of the Nile. (*Bottom right*) Order of Mohammed Ali.

Liberia

The republic of Liberia was founded in 1847 to provide a home for liberated African slaves from the USA.

The Order of the African Redemption was instituted in 1879 (originally known as the Order of the African Liberation), in three classes, as an award for merit for men and women who had given outstanding service to the republic. The medallion of the badge shows an African man and woman kneeling by a cross, while the reverse has the arms of Liberia – a full-rigged sailing ship by a palmtree coast – and the country's motto, THE LOVE OF LIBERTY BROUGHT US HERE.

South Africa

Although the republic of South Africa does not have any Orders, it has instituted a number of decorations.

The highest award is the Castle of Good Hope Decoration, founded in 1965, on the 300th anniversary of the arrival of Jan van Riebeeck in Table Bay. The decoration, in a single class, is awarded for outstanding bravery in action, and is worn round the neck from a sea-green watered ribbon.

Order of the African Redemption : (*Left*) Star ; (*Right*) reverse of the badge.

(*Left*) South Africa : 'Honoris Crux'. (*Right*) Castle of Good Hope Decn. (*Centre*) Zanzibar : Order of El Alijeh.

Jan van Riebeeck is also commemorated by a decoration and a medal which bear his name, for officers and other ranks respectively, for distinguished services in action.

Acts of bravery in action which do not merit the Castle of Good Hope Decoration may be rewarded by the *Honoris Crux* (Cross of Honour), founded in 1952. The badge is in a traditional design, somewhat resembling the Austrian Order of Maria Theresa but with eagles in the angles of the cross.

Other decorations include the Star of South Africa and the John Chard Decoration, the latter named after the officer in charge of the gallant defence of Rorke's Drift in January 1879.

Zanzibar
The Sultanate of Zanzibar, an island off the east coast of Africa, had three orders – the Order of the Brilliant Star, the Order of El Hamoudieh, and the Order of El Alijeh. The last was instituted in 1906 for civil and military merit, in four classes.

AMERICA

United States of America

The United States of America have no orders of knighthood, but there are a number of decorations and an order of merit.

The senior of these is the Medal of Honor, instituted by Congress on 21 December 1861 for the navy, and six months later for the army. Thus it is often known as the Congressional Medal, and is awarded for 'conspicuous gallantry and intrepidity involving risk of life above and beyond the call of duty in action with the enemy'. Originally worn on the left breast, the medal is now worn round the neck.

From 1862 to 1904 the army Medal of Honor was similar in design to that of the navy, but with an eagle and crossed cannon in place of the anchor; the design of the navy medal was changed in 1919, for services in the First World War, to a gold cross *patée* with an anchor on each arm, but in 1942 it reverted to the original design.

The Legion of Merit, closely resembling many foreign orders but ranking as a decoration, was founded in July 1942. There are four degrees – chief commander, commander, officer, and legionnaire – but these are given only to foreigners; for United States service personnel the Legion of Merit is awarded without degree, with the insignia of the fourth class. Both in the style of title and design of the badge, it would seem to owe something to the French Legion of Honour.

Chief commanders wear a large badge as a breast star, while commanders wear a slightly smaller version, with a gilt wreath above it, on a neck ribbon. The two lower grades wear the badge without wreath above, on the left breast, the officer's ribbon having a gilt miniature of the badge on it.

The Distinguished Service Cross is an army decoration, authorized in 1918 and ranking next to the Medal of Honor, for any person serving in the army after 6 April 1917 who distinguishes 'himself or herself by extraordinary heroism against an armed enemy'. The original issue had oak leaves on

Medals of Honor: (*Top left*) Army, 1862; (*Top right*) Army, 1904; (*Bottom left*) Navy, 1917–42; (*Bottom right*) Navy, 1861; (*Centre*) Legion of Merit, Commander's badge.

(*Left*) Army Distinguished Service Cross. (*Right*) Navy Cross.

the arms of the cross, but these were soon dropped for the present design, and the 'oak leaves' type is very rare. If a recipient is cited for a further award of the cross, this is indicated by a bronze oakleaf cluster.

Since 1942 the Navy Cross, established in 1919, takes naval precedence after the Medal of Honor, for acts of extraordinary heroism in action. The dull bronze cross (for a period a grey oxidized metal was used) shows an old sailing ship on the *obv.*, while the *rev.* has crossed anchors between the initials, USN. Second, and subsequent, awards of the cross are indicated by a gold five-pointed star on the ribbon. After the First World War a few British naval officers received this award for distinguished services as at that time the Navy Cross was not purely an award for gallantry in action.

The first US military award for bravery was the Badge of Military Merit, more often called the Purple Heart, and was established by Washington in 1782. It is believed that only three were awarded, all to sergeants, after which the decoration went into disuse. These original awards were not medals,

(*Left*) The Purple Heart. (*Right*) Distinguished Flying Cross.

but the figure of a heart in purple cloth or silk, edged with narrow silver lace or binding, worn on the left breast. Two of the three original awards are still in existence, one of which is embroidered with the word, MERIT, in a wreath.

In February 1932, on the 200th anniversary of Washington's birth, the decoration was revived for award to army personnel (extended in 1942 to the navy, marine corps, and coastguard), for meritorious service and to those wounded in action. In 1942 it was awarded to all US service personnel killed or wounded in action. Although the reverse is inscribed FOR MILITARY MERIT, the decoration can be given for suffering severe frostbite in action.

The original decoration is recalled, not only in the design of the modern Purple Heart, but also in its purple ribbon edged with white.

The Distinguished Flying Cross, instituted in 1926, is awarded to personnel of the army air corps, navy, marine corps, and coastguard, for heroism or extraordinary achieve-

(*Left*) Silver Star. (*Right*) Brevet Medal (Marine Corps).

ment while flying, and was made retrospective to 6 April 1917.

The Medal of Freedom was instituted as an award for civilians for meritorious service in time of war, but has since been extended to cover other outstanding services. Among other awards, it has been presented to the team of *Apollo 13*, after their successful journey to the moon.

In July 1918 an Act of Congress instituted a small five-pointed silver star, 3/16ths of an inch in diameter, to be worn on appropriate medal ribbons to indicate a citation for gallantry in action. This is known as the Citation Star, but in 1932 it was replaced, for the army, by the Silver Star, which is, strangely, a *bronze* five-pointed star with the tiny silver star in the centre; the *rev.* is inscribed, FOR GALLANTRY IN ACTION. This award is not to be confused with the later (1944) Bronze Star, lower ranking, similar in design but with the central star in bronze, and having a red ribbon with narrow white edges and a thin central blue stripe flanked with white.

The Silver Star was extended to the navy in August 1942.

For subsequent awards the army has oakleaf clusters, while the navy has gold stars. The award ranks after the Distinguished Service Medal.

The US Marine Corps has its own decoration, the Brevet Medal (Marine Corps). This was established in 1921 and is awarded to holders of brevet commissions for distinguished service in action. The decoration is a bronze cross *patée*, with the central medallion inscribed, BREVET, surrounded by the title of the corps. The *rev.* is plain apart from the legend, FOR DISTINGUISHED CONDUCT IN PRESENCE OF ENEMY, while the ribbon is unusual, red, embroidered with thirteen white stars, similar to the blue ribbon of the Medal of Honor when that was worn on the breast.

In 1942 a system of unit citations was introduced for US service units, for extraordinary heroism in action. Some British battalions were awarded the Army Citation, and were permitted to wear the decoration – a strip of royal blue ribbon set in a gilt frame of laurel leaves.

Members of 'Apollo 13' Team receiving the Medal of Freedom.

Cuba : Order of Carlos M. de Cespedes (reverse)

Central and South America

From the time of their liberation from the Spanish yoke, in
the first quarter of the nineteenth century, the countries of
Central and South America have frequently experienced the
upsets of revolution, with repeated changes of government.
Many orders and decorations have been established, some of
lasting duration, others ephemeral.

The island of **Cuba**, discovered by Columbus in 1492, was
late in gaining its independence from Spain, becoming a
republic in 1892. The Order of Carlos Manuel de Cespedes was
established in 1926 as a national order of merit in the usual
five classes. Unlike other orders, it has a special sash ribbon
for the President, in five equal stripes, three of blue and two
of white.

For Merit in public health and welfare, the Order of Carlos
J. Finlay dates from 1928, and is named after a doctor who
spent his life fighting yellow fever; perhaps that is why the
colour chosen for the ribbon is a rich yellow.

The national bird of **Guatemala** is the colourful, long

(*Left*) Honduras : Order of Santa Rosa. (*Right*) Guatemala : Order of the Quetzal.

tailed quetzal, in whose honour the national order of merit is named. The Order of the Quetzal is one of the most attractive of Central American orders, and is now in five classes with the badge enamelled in dark and light blue with the bird depicted in all its natural colours.

Honduras claims to be the first landing place on the American mainland by Columbus, in 1502, and was, of course, under Spanish rule until 1821. One of the early Central American orders, founded in 1868, was the Order of Santa Rosa and of Civilization. There were five classes in this award for civil, military, and religious merit, and the nature of the award was indicated on the reverse of the badge, as MERITO CIVIL, MERITO MILITAR, or MERITO RELIGIOSO. Two varieties of the ribbon are found; one has equal stripes of red, blue, white, blue, red, while the other has wide red at each side and narrow blue, white, blue in the centre. The order was abolished in 1901 and it was not until 1941 that it was virtually replaced by the institution of the Order of Francisco Morazan.

(*Left*) Order of the Mexican Eagle (*Note:* the collar has inadvertently been shown inverted). (*Right*) Order of Our Lady of Guadaloupe.

Mexico

From the time when Cortez overthrew the Aztec empire of Montezuma, in 1521, until gaining independence in 1821, Mexico was under Spanish rule. Since then it has had two emperors, Augustin Iturbide (1822–3) and the Austrian Archduke, Maximilian (1863–7), both of whom were dethroned and shot. The first emperor instituted the Order of Our Lady of Guadaloupe in 1822, as an award for civil merit. The colours of the badge – green, white, and red – are the national colours of Mexico and are the basis of the national flag, which also includes the eagle holding a snake, and this is shown, in gold, above the cross of the order. The ribbon, too, is attractive, in a rich deep blue with lilac-pink edges. The order was revived in 1853 by President de Lopez y Santa Anna, and was continued by Maximilian.

Emperor Maximilian founded the Order of the Mexican Eagle in 1865, as the senior order of the empire, in six classes, there being two grades of grand cross, the higher 'with collar'. The badge is unusual, being the eagle holding a green snake in its beak, and a sword and sceptre in its talons. With his Austrian origin, the emperor was obviously influenced by the design of the Austrian Order of the Iron Crown (*q.v.*), the insignia of which is very similar.

In the same year Maximilian instituted the Order of San Carlos, or St Charles, solely for ladies, for works of charity and self-denial, particularly in hospital work. There were two classes; the obverse of the green and white Latin cross was inscribed, HUMILITAS (humility), while the reverse had SAN CARLOS, in Gothic letters.

In modern times, the Order of the Aztec Eagle, dating from 1933, has been instituted for distinguished services by foreigners. The design is unusual and is based on Aztec motifs, with a very stylized eagle and snake; the ribbon is a rich golden yellow – a typical Aztec colour.

(*Left*) Order of the Aztec Eagle. (*Right*) Order of San Carlos.

Argentina

Like the whole of South America (except Brazil), Argentina revolted against Spanish rule early in the nineteenth century, and became independent in 1816. General San Martin was the leader of the war of liberation, and is honoured in the Order of the Liberator San Martin, instituted in 1943 as an award for civil and military merit. His portrait appears on the badge and the star, and the ribbon is in the national colours of pale blue and white.

Another award for civil and military merit is the Order of May (*Orden de Mayo*), created in May 1946. The original designs of the Peron regime – a gold cross quadrate, rayed, with the central medallion showing a young man holding the national flag – was replaced in 1957 by the present design. The ribbon varies according to the division, the civil division being red, and the military, blue, both edged with white.

Argentina also has orders for military, naval, and aeronautical merit, in which the national colours of blue and white predominate in the designs and ribbons.

Bolivia

Declaring its independence from Spain in 1824, the country took the name of Bolivia in 1825, from the liberator, General Simon Bolivar, dictator of Peru. Bolivia is situated up in the Andes, over which the condor flies majestically, so it is not surprising that the order instituted in 1921 for exceptional civil and military merit was given the name of the Order of the Condor of the Andes. The badge, in blue enamel, has clusters of pink trumpet flowers between the arms of the cross, and hangs from a golden condor. The star of the order is similar to the badge, except that the condor is shown on the central medallion.

The Order of Military Merit, created in 1927, also has a blue enamelled cross, but with the figure of an Indian god between the arms; it hangs from a silver condor, but in a conventional representation. There are three classes, and the ribbon is somewhat unusual in that it consists of four equal stripes – two red and two black, giving an unbalanced effect.

Among Bolivian decorations is one for the Battle of Yanacocha, 1835, and a Cross of Honour for the Defence of Chaco.

(*Top left*) Argentina : Order of Mayo. (*Bottom left*) Order of San Martin. (*Top right*) Bolivia : Order of Mil. Merit. (*Bottom right*) Order of the Condor of the Andes.

(*Top left*) Order of Naval Merit. (*Top right*) Imperial Order of the Rose.
(*Bottom*) Imperial Order of the Southern Cross (reverse).

Brazil

For three hundred years Brazil was under Portuguese rule, becoming independent in 1822. But unlike the former Spanish colonies in South America which all became republics, Brazil had an emperor until 1889. In that year, however, the emperor was deposed and the United States of Brazil were established as a republic.

The three ancient Portuguese Orders of Christ, St James of the Sword, and Aviz (*q.v.*) were brought to Brazil when the royal family had to leave Portugal at the end of 1807, owing to Napoleon's invasion. The same insignia were used except that the Crown of Portugal was replaced by the imperial crown, and the plain Portuguese ribbons were given narrow edges, blue for the first two orders and pink for the last.

The Order of the Southern Cross was founded in 1822 by Dom Pedro I, but was discontinued soon after the country became a republic. It was revived in 1932, in a somewhat similar design, but with the imperial portrait and crown replaced by republican insignia; however, the pale blue ribbon and the motto, *Benemerentium praemium*, were retained.

One of the most beautiful orders ever created was the Imperial Order of the Rose, with its rose-pink ribbon with white side stripes. It was founded in 1829, on the marriage of the Emperor to Princess Amelia of Leuchtenberg, as a reward for military and civil merit. The six-pointed star of the badge is set in a wreath of eighteen pink roses with green leaves, and the medallion bears the entwined initials, P, A, surrounded by the motto, AMOR E FIDELIDADE (Love and Fidelity).

In modern times this lovely design has been perpetuated in the Badge of the National Order of Merit, instituted in 1946, and which is almost identical except that the centre shows an armillary sphere or globe in place of the initials and motto.

The Order of Naval Merit, dating from 1934, has an attractive pointed cross with four anchors in the angles, while the Order of Military Merit, founded in the same year, recalls the old Portuguese Order of Aviz in the shape of the cross and in the green of the ribbon. Both orders are in five classes. There is also an Order of Aeronautical Merit, for which the badge has a propellor cross superimposed on a cross potent.

Chilean Order of Merit

Chile

After being a Spanish colony for over two hundred years, Chile revolted against this domination in 1810 and formally declared its independence in 1818. One of the early pioneers of liberty and Chile's first president was Bernardo O'Higgins, and in 1817 he founded the Legion of Merit, particularly to reward those who had distinguished themselves at the battle of Chacabuco. When O'Higgins was deposed in 1823 the award was discontinued, but in 1906 President Riesco revived it as the Order of Merit, for award to foreigners, in six classes – collar, grand cross, grand officer, commander, officer, and caballero (or knight).

Chile was one of the first foreign countries to adopt the Boy Scout movement, and Sir Robert (later Lord) Baden-Powell was awarded the Order of Merit in 1910 – twenty-seven years before he received the British Order of Merit.

Originally the ribbon was in equal stripes of red, white, and blue, but in the modern insignia has a plain blue ribbon.

Colombia

Like Chile, Colombia broke away from Spanish rule, and for a time was united with Venezuela with Simon Bolivar as dictator and, later, as president. He founded the Order of Boyaca as a national order of merit, naming it after the battle of Boyaca, 1819, the final action in the long war for independence. The ribbon is a very distinctive shade of blue with the edges in the colours of the national flag, yellow blue, and red.

In recent times Colombia has instituted the Order of San Carlos for civil and military merit, and the Order of Admiral Padilla for naval merit.

Ecuador

Situated on the equator (hence its name), Ecuador broke away from Colombia in 1830. During the war of independence a young army officer, mortally wounded, became the national hero by his refusal to surrender, and in 1904 an order for military merit was named after him – the Order of Abdon Calderon. The ribbon is in the national colours of yellow, blue, and red.

Ecuador also has Orders of National Merit, Aeronautical Merit, and Agricultural Merit.

(*Left*) Ecuador : Order of Abdon Calderon. (*Right*) Colombia : Order of Boyaca.

(*Left*) Venezuelan Order of Merit. (*Right*) Order of the Sun of Peru.

Peru

The land of the Incas and Pizarro gained its independence in July 1821, and within three months the Order of the Sun was instituted, originally to recognize services rendered in the struggle against Spain. It is awarded in five classes, and both the badge and the star incorporate the multi-rayed design not uncommon in South American awards.

The highest class, a special grand cross, has the star embellished with brilliants. The badge is similar in design to the star but is surmounted by a green and gold laurel wreath, not unlike that of the French Legion of Honour, to which is attached the ring for the plain reddish-brown ribbon.

Venezuela

When the Spaniards landed here in 1499, they named the country Venezuela – Little Venice – from the native houses built on stilts to raise them above the streets of water. After shaking off the Spanish yoke in 1811, the country was linked with Colombia until 1830.

The Order of the Liberator, also known as the Order of the Bust of Simon Bolivar, was founded in 1854, for military and civil merit, and in honour of Simon Bolivar who played such a leading part in the South American struggle for liberty. In the usual five classes, the ribbon shows the national colours of yellow, blue, and red, which are also used by Colombia and Ecuador in their national flags, as all three countries were linked for several years as the state of New Granada.

Venezuela : Order of the Bust of Bolivar : (*Left*) star ; (*Right*) badge.

The insignia of the order varies appreciably, and while in most examples the head is shown to the right, others are found with the head to the left.

The Order of Merit was established in 1861, for both nationals and foreigners, for civil, scientific, and literary merit. There were three classes – grand cross, commander, and knight, with a star for the highest class. The obverse of the badge has the arms of Venezuela, in which the shield is divided into three, with a horse in the bottom half, while the top half is halved, with a sheaf of corn and a pair of crossed flags; the reverse has the date of foundation, 29 August 1861.

Arthur Wellesley, First Duke of
Wellington
Horatio, Viscount Nelson

SOME FAMOUS RECIPIENTS OF ORDERS

Lord Nelson (1758–1805)

Horatio, Viscount Nelson, has always been regarded as one of the most brilliant of British admirals. He quickly rose to his ultimate rank of vice-admiral, becoming a captain at twenty-one and a rear-admiral at thirty-six.

He received the Order of the Bath in 1797, The Order of St Ferdinand and of Merit, of the kingdom of Naples, in 1800, and the Turkish Order of the Crescent in 1802, the last two having been newly created at those times. For his victories at St Vincent and The Nile he also received two of the large Naval Gold Medals (see p. 10).

Although Nelson did not receive many orders, it was his habit of wearing the embroidered stars in action that made him an easy target for the sharpshooter in the rigging of the French ship, *Redoubtable*, at Trafalgar.

The Duke of Wellington (1769–1852)

Arthur Wellesley, 1st Duke of Wellington, was some eleven years younger than Nelson, and had a similar meteoric rise to high rank. He was a lieutenant-colonel at twenty-four and a major-general at thirty-three.

Before he won fame in Portugal and Spain, he had already had considerable military success in India. Much has been written about Wellington's campaigns in the Peninsula and at Waterloo, following which he was inundated with the highest classes of nearly every senior order in Europe. He received the Garter in 1813 and the Grand Cross of the Order of the Bath in 1815.

Among Wellington's many foreign orders – which can all be seen in the magnificent museum at Apsley House, London – are the Golden Fleece (Spanish branch); the Black Eagle and the Red Eagle of Prussia; the Elephant of Denmark; St Andrew, St George, and St Alexander Nevsky, of Russia; the Netherlands Military Order of William; the House Order of Loyalty and the Order of the Zähringen Lion, of Baden; the Rue Crown of Saxony; the French Order of the Holy Spirit; the Hanoverian Guelphic Order; the Tower and Sword, of Portugal, and many others.

Surgeon General William G. N. Manley, VC, CB (1831–1901)

William Manley had the distinction of being the only recipient of both the Victoria Cross and the Prussian Iron Cross.

His extraordinary military career started in 1855 when he was appointed an assistant surgeon, and served with the Royal Artillery Medical Department in the Crimea. He also served in the New Zealand war of 1864–6, where he won the Victoria Cross at the assault of the Gate Pah, tending the wounded under very heavy enemy fire. While in New Zealand, Asst. Surgeon Manley also won the Royal Humane Society's bronze medal for saving an artilleryman from drowning.

During the Franco-Prussian War of 1870–1, Manley served with the British Ambulance in France, where he tended the wounded on both sides, receiving the Prussian Iron Cross (on the white ribbon with black side stripes, for non-combatants), the Bavarian Cross of Merit, and the German war medal, while the French awarded him the Geneva Cross.

Lord Baden-Powell, OM, GCMG, GCVO, KCB (1857–1941)

Robert Stephenson Smyth, 1st Baron Baden-Powell of Gilwell, was undoubtedly one of the outstanding men of our time. Until he was fifty, he was a regular soldier, and captured the imagination of the nation for his defence of Mafeking during the Boer War. Having reached the rank of lieutenant-general, he founded the Boy Scout movement in 1907, as a means of training boys in self-reliance and citizenship through woodcraft and public service.

The scout movement quickly spread throughout the world, and Baden-Powell had many orders and decorations conferred on him. His British awards included the Knight Grand Cross of the Order of St Michael & St George and the Royal Victorian Order, Knight Commander of the Bath and, in 1937, the Order of Merit.

His first foreign award was the Chilean Order of Merit (1910), followed by a score of others including the Order of Christ (Portugal), Dannebrog, Legion of Honour, Oranje-Nassau, the Oak Crown of Luxembourg, the Sword of Sweden.

President Dwight D. Eisenhower (1890–1969)

Known throughout the world as 'Ike', Dwight Eisenhower can be said to have had greatness thrust upon him in middle age. He entered the US army in 1915, as a 2nd Lieutenant of Infantry, and after a career described as 'respectable but not especially brilliant', during which he served on the staffs of Generals McArthur and Marshall, he was eventually appointed Allied Commander-in-Chief, North Africa, in November 1942.

Eisenhower led the allied invasions of Sicily, Italy, and France, and in 1945 he accepted the surrender of Germany. He resigned from the army in 1952, and became the 34th President of the USA.

'Ike' was the recipient of an extraordinary number of foreign orders and decorations. Among these were the Grand Cross of the Bath, Legion of Honour (France), Orders of Victory and Suvorov (USSR), Virtuti Militari and Polonia Restituta (Poland), Lion (Netherlands), Oak Crown (Luxembourg), Leopold (Belgium), Elephant (Denmark), St Olaf (Norway), Southern Cross (Brazil), Aztec Eagle (Mexico), Cloud & Banner (China), George I (Greece), and many others, too numerous to mention.

Mrs Odette Hallowes, GC, MBE

Odette Sansom (now Mrs Hallowes) was the first woman to be awarded the George Cross. A Frenchwoman by birth, her heroic story is well known, and has been perpetuated in the magnificent film, 'Odette', in which Dame Anna Neagle so brilliantly played the title role – how she was sent to the south of France in 1942 with a number of other agents of the Special Operations Executive, and after working for six months with the French Resistance, how she was betrayed and captured by the Gestapo, suffering imprisonment, constant interrogation, and torture for over two years. When she consistently refused to betray her colleagues, she was condemned to death but was eventually liberated from Ravensbruck concentration camp, where she had spent the last months of the war in complete darkness.

Odette (as she is popularly known) was awarded the George Cross in 1946, and the Order of the British Empire. She has also received the Legion of Honour and other awards.

FORMING A COLLECTION

In recent years there has been a large increase in the number of collectors, which is not surprising in view of the attractiveness of orders and decorations. For those who wish to start, it may be helpful to consider how one can set about it.

The first obvious sources of supply are those numismatic dealers whose stocks extend beyond coins. In Britain there are several in London and others can be found in Birmingham, Glasgow, Newcastle-on-Tyne, and elsewhere. Some carry a wide selection of foreign awards, and these, like British orders and decorations, will all be second-hand items. One cannot often buy new insignia in Britain.

On the continent there are not only numismatic dealers but many jewellers who carry stocks, both new and second-hand, of orders and decorations, particularly of their own country. New insignia will probably be expensive and most collectors will prefer to have used examples, especially where the older and obsolete orders are concerned.

(*Below*) scene at a typical medal auction. (*Right*) market stalls can be a useful hunting ground.

Auction sales are another useful source of supply, but the collector is strongly advised to examine the pieces before bidding, to avoid buying damaged or false insignia. In specialist auctions the descriptions of the items are generally reliable, but when an isolated decoration appears in a provincial 'Corn Hall' sale, it is essential to know what one is buying.

But perhaps the most satisfying method of collecting is the genuine hunt for the desired trophies, among the antique shops, junk shops, market stalls, and similar sources. Here the collector must be wary, as the first asking price (especially on the continent) will probably be high but with some hard bargaining a satisfactory purchase may well result. Holidays, both at home and abroad, will provide new hunting grounds, while friends and relations, if suitably approached, may be able and willing to assist in enlarging the collection.

Housing the Collection

As soon as the collector has acquired the nucleus of a collection, he inevitably has to decide how to house or display his treasures. The two most favoured methods are by using wall cases or a cabinet with trays, and each has its advantages and disadvantages.

Wall cases have the advantage of a more spectacular display, permanently on view, but they are expensive to buy new and ribbons are likely to fade (and even rot) by constant exposure to light. Suitable cases can often be bought at local auction sales or second-hand shops; perhaps they originally held butterflies or similar objects, but they can be re-lined with velvet and adapted for decorations.

If a cabinet is favoured, it will be found that it will hold many more specimens, and large trays should be chosen; a very suitable size is 20 in. × 14 in., with a depth of at least $\frac{5}{8}$ in.

It is not difficult to make or adapt a cabinet, provided all the details are well thought out beforehand. For example, the

(*Below*) a typical medal cabinet. (*Right*) Orders can be displayed on a tray or glazed wall case.

medal cabinet should have doors hinged to the front of the
side panels, so that the drawers can come straight out,
whereas other cabinets and cupboards usually have the
doors hinged inside the side panels; this means that either new
doors will have to be fitted or false sides inserted to give the
drawers a clean run. Trays can be lined with velvet or art felt.

The various items are more easily mounted in trays than in
cases, one popular method being by a good quality brass
drawing pin through a narrow strip of stiff cardboard, holding
the folded ribbon to the tray. With wall cases the specimens
should be further held in position by tiny pins at strategic
points to prevent swinging.

For those having suitable accommodation, a glass-topped
show case, such as jewellers use, can make an attractive home
for a small display, changed perhaps from time to time.

MOTTOES AND OTHER INSCRIPTIONS

The following list, by no means exhaustive, may be helpful in identifying insignia, but often mottoes, etc., are shared by two or more orders; also the wording listed may appear only on the star and not on the badge or *vice versa*.

Albertus Animosis   Saxony: O. of Albrecht the Brave

Altior Adversio   Mecklenburg-Strelitz: O. of the Griffin

Aman. Just. Piet. Fid.   Russia: O. of St Anne (Star)

Amor e Fidelidade   Brazil: O. of the Rose

Avita et Aucta   Austria: O. of the Iron Crown

Avito viret Honore   Mecklenburg-Strelitz: O. of Wendish Crown

Benemerentium Praemium   Brazil: O. of the Southern Cross

Caesaris Caesari, Dei Deo   Spain: O. of the Yoke & Arrows

De Rege Optime Merito   Naples: O. of Francis I

Doe Wel en Zie Niet om   Netherlands: O. of the Reunion

Eine Wahrheit, ein Gott, ein Recht   Oldenburg: O. of Duke Peter

Fidei et Merito   Naples: O. of St Ferdinand and of Merit

Fidelitas   Baden: O. of Loyalty

Fideliter et Constanter   Saxe-Ernestine House Order

Fortitudini   Austria: O. of Maria Theresa

Für Badens Ehre   Baden: Military O. of Carl Friedrich

Furchtlos und Trew   Württemberg: O. of the Crown

Für Ehre und Wahrheit   Baden: O. of the Zähringen Lion

Für Verdienst und Treue   Saxony: O. of Merit

Gerechtigkeit ist Macht   Baden: O. of Berthold I

Gott, Ehre, Vaterland   Hesse: O. of Ludwig

Gott und Mein Recht   Württemberg: O. of Friedrich

Honneur et Patrie   France: Legion of Honour

In Fide Salus   Rumania: O. of the Star

In Sanguine Foedus   Naples: O. of St Januarius

Integritate et Merito   Austria: O. of Leopold

Immota Fides   Brunswick: O. of Henry the Lion

Isänmaan Hyvaksi   Finland: O. of the White Rose

Isänmaan Puolesta   Finland: O. of the Cross of Liberty

Je Maintiendrai   Luxembourg: O. of the Golden Lion of Nassau; O. of the Oak Crown. Netherlands: O. of Oranje-Nassau; House O. of Oranje

Ludovicus Mag. Instit. 1693   France: O. of St Louis

L'Union fait la Force – Eendracht maakt Macht: Belgian Orders

Merenti   Bavaria: O. of Military Merit

Nescit Occasum   Sweden: O. of the North Star

Padroeira de Reino   Portugal: O. of Villa Viçosa

Par Teviju   Latvia: O. of the Three Stars

Per Aspera ad Astra   Mecklenburg-Schwerin: O. of Wendish Crown; Latvia: O. of the Three Stars

Praemiando Incitat   Russia: O. of St Stanislas (Star)

Pravda Vitezi   Czechoslovakia: O. of the White Lion

Princeps et Patria   Monaco: O. of St Charles

Pro Fide, Rege, et Lege   Russia: O. of the White Eagle (Star)

Pro Patria   Sweden: O. of the Sword

Quis ut Deus   Bavaria: O. of St Michael

Religion, Independencia, Union   Mexico: O. of Our Lady of Guadaloupe

Sciencias, Letras e Artes   Portugal: O. of St James of the Sword

Si Deus Nobiscum Quis Contra Nos   Hesse: O. of Philip the Magnanimous

Sincere et Constanter   Prussia: O. of the Red Eagle

Suum Cuique   Prussia: O. of the Black Eagle

The Love of Liberty Brought us Here   Liberia: O. of African Redemption

Valor, Lealdade, e Merito   Portugal: O. of the Tower & Sword

Vom Fels zum Meer   Prussia: Royal O. of Hohenzollern

Vigilando Ascendimus   Saxe-Weimar: O. of the White Falcon

Virtus et Honos   Bavaria: O. of Merit of the Bavarian Crown

Virtus Nobilitat   Netherlands: O. of the Netherlands Lion

Virtute   Luxembourg: O. of Adolf of Nassau

Virtute et Fidelitate   Hesse: O. of the Golden Lion

Virtuti et Merito   Papal O. of Pius

Virtuti in Bello   Saxony: Mil. O. of St Henry

Virtuti pro Patria   Bavaria: O. of Max Joseph

Voor Moed, Beleid, Trouw   Netherlands: Mil. O. of William

Za Vitezstvi   Czechoslovakia: Mil. O. of the White Lion

In many cases the letter U is shown as V, in the Latin style. The word, *Verdienst* (Merit), is found on many German and Austrian orders and decorations.

BOOKS TO READ

Although there are relatively few books in English, there is a wealth of literature in foreign languages, and collectors who can read German, French, Spanish, or Italian will find much of interest. Some of the books listed are out of print, but public libraries can usually supply most of them. The following general works are recommended:

The Book of Orders of Knighthood and Decorations of Honour by J. B. Burke, London, 1858.

Collecting Medals and Decorations by Alec A. Purves, London, 1968.

A Handbook of the Orders of Chivalry by C. N. Elvin, London, 1893.

Motti degli Ordini Cavallereschi by C. Padaglione, 3 vols., Naples, n.d. (1907).

Orders and Decorations by Vaclav Mericka, London, 1967.

Orders, Medals, and Decorations of Britain and Europe by Paul Hieronymussen, London, 1967.

Ribbons and Medals by Capt. H. T. Dorling, London, 1963 (revised edition).

Die Ritter- und Verdienstorden, Ehrenzeichen, und Medaillen by L. J. Trost, Vienna, 1910.

Storia degli Ordini Vigenti ed Estinti by E. & D. Guadagnini, Venice, 1925.

In addition to general works there are many hundreds of books dealing with specific countries or groups of countries. The following are just a few examples:

Great Britain: *British Orders and Decorations* by J. C. Risk, New York, 1945.

The Queen's Orders of Chivalry by Sir Ivan de la Bere, London, 1964.

Belgium: *Recueil des Décorations Belges et Congolaises* by H. Quinot, Brussels, 1964 (5th Edition).

France: *Les Ordres Français* by M. Delande, Paris, 1934.

Germany: *Deutsche Orden und Ehrenzeichen* by H. K. Geeb & H. Kirchner, Bonn, 1958.

Japan: *Orders and Medals of Japan and Associated States* by J. W. Peterson, Chicago, 1967.

Netherlands: *Nederlandse Ridderorden en Onderscheidingen* by Dr. W. F. Bax, Rotterdam, 1951.

Scandinavia: *Nordiska Riddarordnar och Dekorationer* by A. Berghman, Malmö, 1949.

Spain: *Condecoraciones Espanolas* by F. de la Puente y Gomez, Madrid, 1953.

SOME MUSEUMS TO VISIT

There are museums in practically every city in the world, and many of these, particularly the military museums, have a collection of orders and decorations. It is impossible to catalogue all these, but the ones listed below are just a few of the many well worth a visit.

Great Britain: Apsley House, Hyde Park Corner, London, W.1. (The Wellington Museum, with all the Duke's orders and decorations, and many other relics).

The Imperial War Museum, Lambeth Road, London, S.E.1.

The Indian Army Museum, Royal Military Academy, Sandhurst, Camberley, Surrey.

The National Maritime Museum, Greenwich, London S.E.

Scottish United Services Museum, Edinburgh Castle.

Australia: Australian War Museum, Canberra.

Czechoslovakia: Historical Military Museum, Prague.

National Museum, Prague.

The State Collection, Orlik Castle.

Denmark: Royal Coin & Medal Collection, Copenhagen.

France: Musée Militaire, Fontainebleau.

Palais de la Légion d'Honneur, Quai Anatole France, Paris.

Jugoslavia: State Museum (formerly the royal palace), Cettinje, Montenegro.

Netherlands: Museum of the Chancery of the Netherlands Orders of Knighthood, Javastraat, The Hague.

The Army Museum, Leiden.

South Africa: South African National War Museum, Johannesburg.

Sweden: Royal Coin Cabinet, Stockholm.

USSR: The Hermitage Museum, Leningrad.

In most county towns and other cities in Britain, there is a regimental museum of the county regiment, while other regiments and corps also have their own regimental museums. While these have mainly collections of medals, they usually also include a number of British and foreign orders and decorations.

ACKNOWLEDGMENTS

The Publishers would like to acknowledge the assistance given to them by the following:

Exhibition Department, Imperial War Museum, London

Press Section, United States Embassy, London

RAMC Museum, Keogh Barracks, Ash Vale, Hants

Medals Department, Spink & Son Ltd., London

The family of the late Signor F. Matania, Rome

INDEX

Page numbers in bold type refer to illustrations.

General Index

Index of Countries

Index of Principal Orders